Monica Porter was b............................gary in 1952, the daughter of two well-known figures in the Hungarian artistic world: the writer, Péter Halász, and the singer, Vali Rácz. Her family emigrated to America when she was four. She was brought up in New York, then came to London in 1970 to study acting, and has lived here ever since.

She has been a freelance journalist for several years, contributing to a variety of newspapers and magazines, as well as writing and broadcasting programmes for the BBC. *Dreams and Doorways* is her third book.

She lives in Maida Vale, London, with her two sons.

MONICA PORTER

DREAMS AND DOORWAYS

*Turning points in the early lives
of famous people.*

PAN

First published 1993 by Pan Macmillan Children's Books

a division of Pan Macmillan Publishers Limited
Cavaye Place London SW10 9PG
and Basingstoke

Associated companies throughout the world

ISBN 0–330–32634–1

1 3 5 7 9 8 6 4 2

A CIP catalogue record for this book is available from
the British Library

Typeset by Intype, London
Printed by Cox & Wyman Ltd, Reading

For my sons, Adam and Nicky

Contents

Introduction

othing which happens to us during the years of our childhood is ever lost. Those early experiences, both good and bad, provide the most potent raw material of our future lives, the material out of which our achievements are forged. Everything that we see and feel, that we absorb as children, has its echo and its effect somewhere further along the line.

'The childhood shows the man, as morning shows the day,' wrote the seventeenth-century poet, John Milton. Our adult behaviour and actions usually have their origins in the various formative elements of our childhood and adolescence. It often takes a very long time for us to understand (and sometimes we never understand completely) just how our early years shape the rest of our lives. Often it isn't until middle age, or even old age, that we can clearly see the significance of those early episodes and events, and evaluate the places where we grew up and the people we grew up with.

It is often the little things, the small details, rather than the grand sweep of our lives, which leave the deepest marks. And although we might think we are masters of our destiny, it can easily be some fluke which determines the course of our future lives, or a series of flukes. Our turning points can be marked by a dramatic event or something which seems minor at the time; they come about either by accident or design.

It's encouraging to note how frequently the successes and satisfactions of adulthood can be traced back to an origin of pain, hardship and disappointment in childhood. Our greatest strengths are often forged out of what we might consider 'bad luck' in our early lives. Likewise, privileged and pampered children can grow into failed and dismally unhappy adults – the 'easy life' isn't always as easy as one supposes. Again, we need the benefit of hindsight in order to decide what was ultimately lucky or unlucky in our childhood.

One is never again quite so receptive to the external world as during the years of childhood, when the future adult is being formed. Our senses are at their freshest and sharpest, everything has the attraction of the new. This is when we establish our all-important mental 'databank' into which we put our experiences and observations. It's vital to be open to the world, to observe and absorb as much of life as we can. Nothing goes astray. Everything is stored away somewhere in the databank, and everything is of potential worth.

The celebrated men and women in this book have looked back upon their beginnings and found their decisive moments, their visions and inspirations, the twists and turns of their youth. Along with their memories, both poignant and happy, and their light-hearted anecdotes, they offer some valuable pointers to the youngsters of today.

If the child determines the adult, and adults determine the future of our world, one thing is pretty clear: being a child isn't just kids' play, it's an important occupation, too.

Sir James Savile, OBE

'Ideas which are considered wild and foolish when one is penniless suddenly become brilliant in the eyes of the world as soon as one starts to make money.'

Born in Leeds on 31 October 1926. Education: St Anne's Elementary School, Leeds. Career: Disc Jockey, radio and television personality, voluntary hospital worker, charity fundraiser.

small, sickly baby, the youngest of seven, Jimmy Savile nearly died at the age of two. But God – the 'Boss', as Jimmy calls him – wasn't ready for him yet. As his grandma bent over him with a mirror to see if he was still breathing, Jimmy peed into her eye.

'I continued throughout my infancy to pee on anything or anyone within range . . . guests, fires, teatables, priests and other such targets. I wasn't very popular for a number of years.'

He was small and weak until, at twelve, he obtained his first bicycle, which became his constant companion and was his 'passport to health and strength'. As a young man he developed into a cyclist of international racing standard: 'In those days there were no cars on the roads, no motorways, and the whole country was a giant fairy kingdom. A week's holiday would see me off on my own around Scotland and I would cover well over 1000 miles.'

His cycling proficiency foreshadowed his many famed charity walks and runs as a celebrity. But long before this he had another forte in life: the dance-hall business. It really all began when young Jimmy had his first taste of the night-life at the Mecca dance hall in Leeds, where he worked after school hours as a general dogsbody – a job which qualified him for 'every A level that ever existed in hell . . . I was everyone's mascot, pet, runner and holder of mysterious parcels and secrets. Because I didn't understand the first thing about anything I was the confidant of black marketeers and crooks of every trade.'

His knowledge of the world expanded when, at the age of twelve, he had his first date with a 'real girl' – the dance-hall cashier, who was about twenty. He was the envy of all. 'As I only ever saw the top ten per cent of her through the glass, it never occurred to me that there was a bottom part.' They went to the cinema, and there, in the darkness, he discovered that 'the ninety per cent you can't see is as important as the ten per cent you can'.

His adolescent years continued to centre around the dance hall, that strange adult world which so baffled him. During the war the dance hall employed a female band, since all the men were being sent off to fight. Jimmy was paid ten shillings a week to play the drums during the half-hour interval – illegally, of course, as he was under age. When the nightly air-raid sirens sounded he'd rush up to the roof to see where the latest local fires were and report back. Yankee soldiers arrived and frequented the dance hall, often leaving behind their packs of cigarettes – as precious as gold dust in those days – which Jimmy would find and give to a grateful night-watchman. The war was a constant source of excitement for him.

He left school and the dance hall behind at fourteen and spent a couple of years doing office work, supplementing his income by winning at card games during the lunch-break. The dance-hall experience had made him an expert in dealing from every part of the deck. But: 'It never occurred to me to take any more than I might need for an evening's enjoyment or to subsidize a penniless friend from the other players – just as crooked as me but not nearly as good.'

As the war progressed he was called up. He would have liked to follow his two great heroes, his brothers John and Vincent, into the navy. But as he couldn't swim, the navy was out. He was still too weak to join the army; it was obvious that just wearing the regulation boots would have kept him 'permanently welded to the floor'. He fancied being a rear gunner in the RAF, but his eyesight wasn't up to scratch, and 'the RAF felt that I could be of more use to the British war effort if I was loaned to the enemy'.

So, at sixteen, he became one of the 'Bevin boys' – conscripts chosen to work in the coalmines – under the scheme launched by the Minister of Labour, Ernest Bevin. So began six years of dirty, dark and dangerous work in the bowels of the earth. More than once he had near-misses with death; it seemed that the 'Boss' was still not ready to welcome him through the heavenly gates. He also suffered various indignities, such as his working partnership with a constantly farting pit pony.

Then an incident occurred which was to alter the course of his life. He was down the mine one day 'belt-cleaning' – shovelling coal dust off the conveyor belt. Not realizing that the coal seam near him was about to be exploded, he was caught by the blast. 'The man who detonates the shot looks down the face to check that no lights, the miner's constant friend, are visible. No one had told me of this hazard and my light happened to be on the wrong side of the belt.'

Miraculously, although covered in debris, he didn't seem to be seriously hurt. He had some aches and pains, but within a few days they disappeared – all except the pain in his back, which grew worse. In the end he was fitted with a surgical corset, given walking sticks, and with sixteen shillings a week sick money he was released from his Bevin boy duties, a free man at last.

For a while he stayed at home, lay in bed, and was looked after by his adored Mum whom he calls 'the Duchess'. But he wasn't happy doing that for long. He was ambitious. He wanted to make money. To inspire him, he pinned a picture of a Rolls Royce on the inside of his wardrobe door. 'None of our family had ever possessed a motorbike let alone a car, but a picture would do for a start.'

One day he heard that a friend of his had concocted a strange machine from the innards of an old radio. When connected to a wind-up gramophone, it produced music on a very grand scale. It was, in effect, the first electric amplifier. He and his friend struck a business deal, immediately organizing an evening of 'fantastic entertainment' for a one-shilling admission fee in a hired hall. Their mothers were commissioned to produce the refreshments.

'Installing the equipment was fraught with dangers. It was in several pieces connected by wires. These covered the top of a grand piano, glowed red hot when switched on for

4

longer than five minutes, and charred the top of that noble instrument for the rest of its days. By nine p.m. we had taken eleven shillings, the machine had melted at several soldered points and died quietly, but not before giving a final shock to its inventor, causing him to weep openly.'

This disaster notwithstanding, the evening was applauded by all, and Jimmy and his friend pocketed five shillings and sixpence each. 'And thus the world's first disco, as they have come to be called, took place in the top room of the Belle Vue Road branch of the Loyal Order of Ancient Shepherds.'

It was a whole new concept: public dancing to amplified recorded music, as opposed to live bands. Jimmy began to market his innovation, trudging around with his 'infernal machine' from one makeshift dance venue to another. Sometimes only a dozen people would turn up and the taxi fare home would cost more than he'd made at the door. He decided that he needed to acquire business expertise.

And that's how he came full circle, taking a job as assistant manager of the same Mecca dance hall in Leeds where he'd worked as a schoolboy. It was a world he knew and understood. Before long his idiosyncratic approach and highly effective publicity stunts were being noticed at Mecca's head office in London. He was on the road to becoming their award-winning star dance-hall manager . . . and the owner of a *real* Rolls Royce.

It was at Mecca's Ilford dance hall that Jimmy, as manager, introduced his highly popular discos. 'Ideas which are considered wild and foolish when one is penniless suddenly become brilliant in the eyes of the world as soon as one starts to make money.' The Mecca directors couldn't argue with Jimmy's success, although they warned their other managers not to follow his maverick example. One of him was enough.

From Ilford he was sent to run the Plaza dance hall in Manchester, then back to Leeds. It was there that by chance he acquired his most distinctive trait: his bleached blond hair. 'Some juniors from a ladies' hair salon were dance regulars and asked me if I'd like a free hairdo. It was student practice night so I suggested they should turn me into a raving blond. A cold goo was slapped on to my unsuspecting head and I was left to cook.' The fledgling hairdressers, however, got the mixture wrong and poor Jimmy was in agony as the strong chemicals ate into his scalp.

His reappearance at the dance hall as a blond was dramatic. It was also very good for business. So for the several weeks following his hair colour changed constantly, culminating in an elaborate tartan display which took six hours to create. After the shock of seeing it nearly caused a man to pass out on a train, Jimmy decided to go back to being a plain old bleached blond.

His big break into the media came when the Radio Luxembourg disc jockey, Pat Campbell, wandered into the hall one night and was astounded by the vibrant atmosphere created by the blond apparition on stage. He was convinced that Jimmy was a natural for popular radio. Six months later, in 1958, he had his own show on Radio Luxembourg. The air waves were never the same again. Radio led to television: in 1964 he became the first *Top of the Pops* presenter, and his crazy on-screen antics were soon famous throughout Britain.

Despite fame and wealth, he has carried on with his long-standing voluntary work as a hospital porter. It has kept him in touch with the other side of life, the side which he remembers so well from his humble childhood days in Leeds.

Although what his patients make of being wheeled into an operating theatre by a 'mature' DJ with a shock of bleached blond hair, the Boss only knows!

Terry Pratchett

'Luckily, I was the kind of kid who could get through science by writing a poem about what it feels like to be a plutonium atom.'

Born in Beaconsfield, Buckinghamshire, on 28 April 1948. Education: Holtspur County Primary School, High Wycombe Technical High School. Career: Novelist; books include: *The Colour of Magic*, *The Light Fantastic*, *Equal Rites*, *Mort*, *Wyrd Sisters*, *The Dark Side of the Sun*, *Truckers*, *Diggers*, *Strata*.

ntil I was ten my family lived in a house with one cold tap and an outside lavatory. After the Second World War you lived in any property you could get your hands on. I was an only child. My father was a highly skilled motor mechanic; he could put his ear to an engine and know exactly which bit to repair. My mother's jobs always involved accountancy – she is very good with numbers. She's as close to a Jewish mother as it's possible to get while being a hundred per cent gentile, by which I mean that she had a great respect for education, and always encouraged me to read and learn. I was the only one in my class to pass the eleven-plus exam.

'Like many other kids of my generation and from a similar background, my parents brought me up to a certain level and I took off from there. I've a lot of respect for them, they're both very bright. If they had been able to take advantage of the existing educational opportunities themselves, they would have gone on to greater things.

'From the age of nine or ten I wanted passionately to be an astronomer. This went on for several years, mainly because it meant I could stay up late looking through a telescope. My dad made a tripod for it, and I'd be out on freezing cold nights mapping the surface of the moon. But as I grew older I realized that most astronomy really meant sitting in a shed in Cambridge doing maths – today nearly *all* science is sitting in a shed somewhere doing maths.

'What I really had was a kind of vague interest in the universe. The space age was just beginning, and I realize now that I was showing a *journalistic* interest in it. It's great being a journalist, because you're allowed to dip into lots of things without having to get all the qualifications necessary to do them.

'I didn't want to learn Latin, which I'd have had to do at grammar school, so I chose technical school instead, where you could get your hands dirty with "technical" subjects, like woodwork. It was a stupid decision, the first real mistake of my life.

'I hated secondary school. Nothing seemed to have any relevance. The first two or three years were hellish. I got through three years of O level maths without the teacher ever finding out that I couldn't do quadratic equations. I might have got a grip on it, if someone had only taken half an hour to explain it without throwing any chalk at me. Luckily, I was the kind of kid who could get through science by writing a poem about what it feels like to be a plutonium atom.

'I always felt that school got in the way of my real *education*, which was my reading. *The Wind in the Willows* was the first book to really nail me to the floor, when I was ten – it introduced me to the world of really well-written fantasy. After that I devoured books. My record was forty library books in one week. I used to help out in the local library in Beaconsfield on Saturday afternoons, so that I could write myself out as many tickets as I wanted. I also cycled every week to a second-hand bookshop in a neighbouring village, and came home with *bags* of stuff, like bound volumes of *Punch* from 1900 for half a crown, and all the old classic humorists. I tore through the stuff like a chain-saw.

'Sports, on the other hand, I couldn't stand. That came from being constantly shouted at by a mad Welsh sports master. The only sport I liked was hockey, because they gave you a stick. After two years of rugby, in which I was beaten up by big kids, it was a real relief to play hockey. The big kids found out that there's nothing worse than a small kid with a stick and a grudge.

'When I was thirteen our English teacher, at a loss for what to do one day, told us to write a short story. I wrote one, and she gave me twenty out of twenty for it. (The only other thing I'd ever got twenty out of twenty for was a picture of two dinosaurs fighting.) It was put into the school magazine.

'The story was about how the Devil, upset that no one is being sent to hell anymore because of all the salvation going on, decides to hire an advertising agency to convince people to go to hell voluntarily. The advertising agent is very pleased to get this commission, which is the only one he has, but his problem is to find a way to promote hell without getting on the wrong side of God.

'Actually, the teachers were quite brave to bung it into the magazine. All the kids liked it. But the headmaster made some very strange comments about the magazine in assembly, and it became apparent that he disapproved of the "moral content" of my story. I never liked the headmaster – we were two people who instinctively didn't get on. He's still alive, so I have to be careful what I say. Anyway, that taught me something about the power of the written word.

'I rewrote the story, tidied it up a bit, got my aunt to type it for me and sent it to a well-known magazine called *New World Science Fiction*, which promptly accepted it and sent me fourteen pounds. Then, in the best traditions of the market economy, the first thing I did was to sack my aunt and buy myself a used typewriter. My mum was so impressed that I'd invested the money in my future writing that she paid for me to take a touch-typing course.

'Having something that you know you're good at is incredibly useful, and my last few years at school were much better. In what was a fairly bewildering world, I'd actually found someplace where I could stand and say, "Right – *this*, at least, is solid!" So that was a major turning point. I suspect that if I hadn't sold the first story I ever wrote I might never have written another word. I'd have thought: oh well, this writing business is not for me, and done something else.

'When I was seventeen I wrote to the editor of our local paper, the *Bucks Free Press*, and told him that I would be leaving school the following year and hoped to get a certain number of A levels and what were the chances of a job for me then? He wrote back saying he had an opening for a trainee at the moment. I went to see him and was offered the job. My parents were on holiday at the time, and when they returned I told them I wanted to quit school and take the job, which meant giving up my A levels. And, God bless them, they accepted it quite calmly. They weren't entirely happy about it, but they didn't stand in my way because they knew it wasn't just a "dead-end job", that it could lead to a zillion things. It gave you freedom to manoeuvre.

'One of the best days of my life was when I went to school on the first day of the next term, with all my schoolbooks in a bag, and just left them there. The headmaster was really glad to see me go.

'It's likely that today you'd need a college education before being offered a job like that. But in those days the editor only had to make sure that I had a good academic record up until that point. As it was, by the time I was twenty-one, I could have edited my own newspaper, I had genuine skills.'

Terry worked as a journalist for many years. His first book, *The Carpet People*, was published in 1971, and every few years after that he'd produce a new book which did quite nicely. But *The Colour of Magic*, published in 1985, propelled him into a new realm of success – it was the first in his Discworld series, the stories that take place on a flat world which 'rides on the back of four giant elephants who stand on the shell of the enormous star turtle Great A'Tuin, and which is bounded by a waterfall that cascades endlessly into space.

'A lot of the humour in the Discworld books comes from applying logic to situations which don't, on the whole, stand up under logical examination. For example, if Death is that bony character with the scythe, what does he actually *do*? Since the answers don't exist, you have to make them up, to provide the "details" – it's all part of the same inquisitive, journalistic mentality, which I suppose I already had when I wrote that first story in school.

'What I always look for is a *kick*, something to tickle the sense-of-wonder nodes. It can be found in just about everything, in the real world as well as in fantasy and science fiction. And the commonplace, everyday "miracles" of life are often far more amazing than fantasy. There's nothing so wonderful about a wizard making fire appear, because that's what wizards do. But when you think of all the necessary factors that our civilization has to bring together in order to make a streetlight come on – now that's *far* more wonderful.

'I think our brains contain a damper mechanism which cuts out our sense of wonder about things, otherwise we'd all be going around like hippies, saying "Wow, man!" at everything. The sheer weirdness of the world would over-whelm us if we didn't have the ability to shut it out.'

Terry refuses to shut it out, knowing very well that it is precisely his acute sense of wonder at our weird world which inspires his writing.

'What's my advice to kids today? Stay "alive". There are a lot of people out there who have died, even though they're still walking around. The mouth moves and the eyes open and shut, but they've switched off.'

Edina Ronay

'I dyed the regulation navy-blue coat a sort of *off* navy-blue – I recall the headmistress holding it up to the light in her office, to examine the unorthodox tint.'

Born in Budapest, Hungary. Education: Our Lady of Sion, Bayswater, London; Putney High School for Girls; St Martin's School of Art; RADA. Career: Former actress and model; fashion designer since 1979.

hen, soon after World War II, the communists installed their dictatorships in the countries of Eastern Europe, many people chose to leave their homes and head towards the West and freedom. Among them was the Ronay family of Budapest. Egon Ronay, like his father and uncle, had been a wealthy restaurateur there. With his wife and two small daughters, he decided to begin a new life in England.

He eventually became a household name as a restaurant critic and general food expert – *Egon Ronay's Good Food Guide* was the bible consulted by every self-respecting gourmet before going out to eat. The story of a successful *émigré*, if ever there was one.

Edina was four when she arrived in England, after a train journey from Budapest during which she'd been constantly sick. (It put her off trains for life.) Within months, barely noticing the transition, she and her elder sister Esther spoke fluent English. Today Esther is an independent film producer, and Edina one of Britain's top names in fashion design.

Clothes were an important feature in the lives of the two little girls. Edina explains: 'My mother was always beautifully dressed, very stylish. In Budapest she wore only couture clothes, like all well-to-do women there. After we came to England, she naturally could no longer afford that, but she didn't let her standards of appearance drop. And she fussed a great deal over our clothes, too. My sister and I had matching dresses made, exquisitely hand-embroidered. We were made to wear white gloves when we went somewhere special. We were always being hauled off to the dressmakers – it was a real nuisance. But it instilled in me a taste for good-quality, well-made clothes. I could never stand shoddy garments.'

Her 'formal, bourgeois' parents sent her to Putney High School, which she didn't like. 'It was big and impersonal, and I didn't find the other girls too inspiring. The only thing there which excited me was the art. I was never really academic – I was far more interested in boys (I was always falling in love with some boy for about a minute) and dancing. I was mad about jiving, and won a lot of jiving competitions.

'Elvis Presley was my big hero and my parents were worried because I was always going to jive clubs and playing rock and roll records. They said that unless I went once a week to an opera or ballet, I couldn't listen to Elvis. So I'd stay for the first half of some performance at the Royal Albert Hall and then quickly escape to the local clubs. I developed a long-standing dislike of opera because of my parents' insistence that I go to them.

'I loved going to coffee bars – the really "in" thing at the time – which were usually in Soho. That was the hub of bohemian life in London in the fifties. I also went to the Mardi Gras in South Kensington, where the teenagers from the French Lycee used to congregate. I made lots of friends there, and went to lots of parties.

'My own school was boring and staid. I always wanted to be different from the other girls, who were rather conventional.' Not overtly mutinous, Edina asserted her independence through subtle deviation from the drab school uniform. 'I wore my cardigan back-to-front. I carried my bag in a different way to everyone else. I dyed the regulation navy-blue coat a sort of *off* navy-blue – I recall the headmistress holding it up to the light in her office, to examine the unorthodox tint. And I always took the hat off the moment I left school, which made my sister's life difficult, because she was a prefect and her job was to make sure I kept the hat on. Unlike me, she was serious and academic – the one with the intellectual friends.

'I always tried to get out of sports, netball and things like that, because I hated to go outside when it was cold wearing a stupid pair of shorts. I used to forge letters from my father (he still doesn't know about that), saying, "I'm terribly sorry but Edina is ill today." I was naughty, but I was never really bad.'

She couldn't wait to leave school. After O levels, her impressive art portfolio got her into St Martin's School of Art. 'I was only sixteen – the youngest one there. I loved every minute of it. I met all kinds of bizarre, arty people, with weird hairdos and incredible clothes – a great relief from the straight pupils at Putney. I personally modelled myself completely on the French film star Brigitte Bardot, whom I actually resembled at the time. I wore a beehive hairdo and tight skirts, had pouting white lips and masses of eye make-up.'

Before she even finished her first year at art school, she was 'discovered'. 'I was walking down Tottenham Court Road one day when a film producer stopped me and said he wanted me to be in his film. We talked about it over coffee. Nothing ever came of it, but I decided to leave college and become an actress. My parents weren't too happy about this; they began to wonder whether I'd ever settle down to *anything*. But they knew it would be useless protesting. My father helped me acquire an agent, I had publicity photos taken, and I began to get small acting parts.

'My first good part was as one of the sixth-formers in *Pure Hell at St Trinians*, which was shot at Shepperton Studios. Cary Grant was there doing another film, and he gave me and another of the girls a lift home each evening in his chauffeur-driven limousine, which was most exciting!'

After a couple of years of acting, her father persuaded her to enrol in the Royal Academy of Dramatic Arts. She completed only two-thirds of the course when she was asked to leave. 'The Principal disapprovingly told me that I was more suited to the "secondary arts" – films and television – as opposed to the theatre. We had a big argument because, unlike him, I didn't think they *were* secondary.'

Her boyfriend in those days was a struggling young actor called Michael Caine, then sharing digs with his friend Terence Stamp (who was going out with top model Jean Shrimpton). 'It was all very *sixties*, we had a wonderful time. I was forever "up-and-coming", and about to become the "new face of the times" or whatever. But then I met my future husband, we went travelling, and I left all that behind.'

Back in London a year later, she found the British film industry in the doldrums, so she started to model. This led to a more intense interest in clothes. She began to buy antique clothes (all the rage at the time) and re-vamp them to sell to friends, then to design unusual knitwear. She finally opened her own shop on the King's Road in 1979, and since then has established a thriving international fashion business. The sense of chic and meticulousness which she absorbed from her mother has paid off.

She may have left her native country as a small child, but her cultural identity is still strong, and she returns frequently. 'Hungarians are very vibrant people, and they love vivid colours. I think the grey English climate produces a greyer national character. You can tell from the clothes I design that I'm not English, not only because I often incorporate traditional Hungarian folk styles, but also from the far more interesting use of colours.'

Henry Cooper, OBE

'Our heroes weren't pop stars or soap opera stars, in those days before television, they were the great boxers, and we listened to all the fights on the radio.'

Born in Camberwell, south-east London, on 3 May 1934. Education: Athelney Street School, Bellingham. Career: Professional boxer from 1954–71. British and Commonwealth heavyweight champion from 1959–71. Six times European champion. Company director since 1972. BBC radio boxing commentator.

e were a working-class family from south-east London: my mum and dad – bless their hearts – my older brother and my twin brother George. My dad came from a boxing family – he boxed in the army, and *his* father, my grandfather, was an old bare knuckle fighter. So we grew up listening to stories about grandad and the old bare knuckle days. George and I took to boxing like ducks to water.'

Sitting in Henry Cooper's spacious and immaculate house in the north London suburb of Hendon, his cleaning lady hoovering in a distant room, his big wire-haired terrier ('Don't worry – he likes females') lying on top of my right foot, it all seemed a long way from the humble early days Henry is describing.

'My dad was a London tram driver . . : until he knocked a copper off his bike and was demoted to conductor. He'd been a boy soldier at the end of the 1914–18 war, then when the Second World War came, he was sent to Burma and India for four years. That was a tough time for Mum, bringing us up on her own. She was out cleaning offices early in the morning, then during the day she worked as a dinner lady at our school. (George and I always got extra big portions.) Us kids all had jobs, too – we had our paper rounds, we helped the milkman. We all had to earn money from the age of eight or nine, to help keep us going. At the end of the week we'd give the money to Mum.

'Sometimes there was only bread and dripping for tea, but whatever there was, the family always sat down and had a meal together each evening. There was none of this "give the kid a quid to go out for a hamburger" type of thing you get today. Family values have broken down. And all the nonsense they talk now about not smacking your kids. We got plenty of wallops from our Mum, but we always knew we'd deserved it, and we didn't love her any the less. It broke our hearts when she died.'

Henry and his identical twin George always had a very close, supportive relationship. They were both sparring partners and best friends. 'You're never lonely as a twin. We were always together – we went to school together, we started boxing together with the same trainer, we did our National Service in the Army together (in a boxing battalion). We only separated when I got married in nineteen fifty-nine.'

The other kids at school couldn't tell the twins apart. If one of them got into trouble with a bigger boy and got collared, he'd say, 'No, it's not me you want – it's my brother!' So then the boy would get hold of the other twin, who'd plead, 'No, you want my brother, not me!' And it would carry on like this until the whole business fizzled out.

'Academically, I'm a dummy. I hated school, especially arithmetic. We went to school during the war years. We were hoping and praying the school would be bombed, and when it wasn't, we set it alight. There was a whole gang of us and someone put a match to a stack of waste paper kept under the stairs. The headmaster had to be rescued from his office right above the stairs.

'Schooling was the last thing we wanted. We just wanted to get out and work and start earning some money. We weren't worried about being clever.'

He and George left school at fifteen, but not before they'd won several regional schoolboy boxing championships. They began to show real potential by about the age of fourteen, already toughened up by the Bellingham Amateur Boxing Club.

Did his parents encourage him in his ambition? 'Oh, yes. Coming from working-class people, and especially in that part of south London where my family was, around Bermondsey and the Elephant and Castle – which was steeped in boxing history, with the old Blackfriars Ring and all of that – boxing was a major thing in people's lives. Our heroes weren't pop stars or soap opera stars, in those days before television, they were the great boxers, and we listened to all the fights on the radio. Our favourite was the American Joe Louis – world heavyweight champion in the thirties and forties, when I was a kid. He was my idol.'

(It was the black Joe Louis, nicknamed the 'Brown Bomber', who really opened up professional boxing as a sport to black fighters. In 1938 he fought the famous German boxer Max Schmeling and knocked him out in two minutes flat. Hitler, who hated black people as much as he hated Jews, was furious.)

'Good boxers, good fighters, come from deprived working-class areas. They don't come from the pampered middle class, the public school- and university-educated. Boxing has to be *in the blood*, a man has to feel that desperation to fight his way out of poverty and hopelessness. For lots of young working-class men, boxing has always been the only possible route to a better life.' He berates those brain surgeons who sit in their posh Harley Street surgeries calling for the sport to be banned. 'Everyone knows it has its dangers, but so does crossing the street.'

Amateur boxing had a great deal to offer kids. 'It's all about discipline. You need discipline in the gym, in training, and in the ring. You have to have discipline as a way of life, too. If you want to be a good boxer, you can't go to parties, you can't go boozing and dancing. So it teaches you something fundamental, which you then apply to other areas of your life.' It also channelled the physical energy inherent in young males into an organized and controlled activity. 'Boxers are the least aggressive people you can meet. If you've been in the gym for two hours working out, you don't hang around street corners looking for a fight. George and I were always easy-going. It took an awful lot to get us rattled. As kids, we'd sooner run away from trouble.'

Ironically, Henry's success has meant that there will be no fourth generation of boxers in the Cooper family. He was an established professional earning good money when he married and moved out of that tough south London environment where boxing was king. His own two sons were 'raised in luxury. They had everything – all the computer games, you name it.' But they had no inclination to box.

On my way out I stopped to gaze at the massive glass-fronted cabinet, stretching the full length of the wall, crammed with Henry's gleaming trophies, medals and awards.

What was the most glorious moment of his career? Perhaps that time back in 1964 when he was in the ring with Cassius Clay (later known as Muhammad Ali), and floored the cocky young American with the famous left hook they called 'Henry's Hammer'? It was one of the most celebrated blows in British boxing history.

'No. The high point for me was when I went to Buckingham Palace to receive the OBE from the Queen. Boxing for me has opened a million doors: I've been all over the world, I've been to the Olympic games, I've had breakfast at two in the morning at Buckingham Palace and I've had lunches with prime ministers at 10 Downing Street . . . '

And I'll bet it wasn't bread and dripping.

Bonnie Langford

'Noel Coward was in the audience, too, and his famous comment after the show was, "Cut the second act and the child's throat". *I* was the child he was referring to.'

Born in Hampton Court, Surrey, on 22 July 1964. Education: St Catherine's Convent School, Twickenham; Arts Educational School and Italia Conti Stage School, London. Career: Actress. Stage roles include: Bonnie Butler in *Gone with the Wind*, Baby June in *Gypsy*, Rumpleteazer in *Cats*, Peter Pan, Cinderella. TV roles include: Violet Elizabeth in *Just William*, Melanie in *Dr Who*.

Rarely does fame come as early in life as it did for Bonnie: she's been a professional performer since the age of seven. Even rarer, she's still going strong in her late-twenties. The careers of most child stars fizzle out as they grow up, because they lose their 'star quality' in the process. Bonnie is an exception to the rule.

'My mother had been a dancer, and her family had dancing in the blood – her aunt was a ballerina in Anna Pavlova's company, and had a dancing school which my mother later took over. I first learnt to dance at my mother's school. My two older sisters both became professional ballerinas. So ours was a very "girly" household in which dance training from an early age was an important feature. My father had nothing to do with the business at all. He ran a leather goods company, was very stable and kept us all down to earth.

'I was a placid child, tidy and organized and level-headed. From three to six I attended our local convent school, as was the tradition in my family. My mother had been there, and my nieces go there now. I would have continued there, except that my life changed at six, when a friend of ours put my name forward for the TV talent contest *Opportunity Knocks*.

'The auditions were held in Teddington, near my home. There was an enormous number of people trying out for the show – pop groups, a man playing a song on spoons – it was all a bit ridiculous. I very nearly left before I was called to do my number. I wasn't fazed or nervous; I took it all matter-of-factly. It was no big deal to me whether I appeared on the show or not.

'I was about to leave when Hughie Green, the host, turned to me and asked whether I wanted to go on next. I got up and launched into my song: *'On the Good Ship Lollipop'*. He stopped me halfway through, then told me to start again while he taped me. That, apparently, was what they did with anyone who they thought had a good chance.

'A few weeks later a letter arrived to say I'd made it on to the show. My father took me to the studio to record my number. They'd built a special set for me with a flight of very steep stairs which I had to walk down, and they told me to watch the red light above the camera. I'd brought a little costume with me, but they said I should sing in the clothes I had on – a pair of black velvet hot-pants.

'I won the contest, and was meant to go back the following week and repeat my performance, as the winner does, but I didn't go. It was the week of the show put on by my mother's dancing school. I was in it, and didn't want anything to disrupt that. So they gave the winning spot to somebody else. I didn't think twice about it.'

The following year she was given the part of Bonnie in the musical version of *Gone with the Wind*, at London's Drury Lane Theatre. She was chosen from thousands of aspirants, along with the four other girls with whom she alternated in the role – doing two performances a week each. (Strict British laws governing the work hours of child actors meant it was impossible for one child to play the part alone.)

'I was chosen to play on the opening night, in the presence of Princess Anne. Noel Coward was in the audience, too, and his famous comment after the show was, "Cut the second act and the child's throat". *I* was the child he was referring to. My parents were really hurt by that quote and made sure it didn't reach me, but when I heard about it some years later I had to laugh; I thought it was very funny.

'The horse and I got all the publicity in that show. The horse "performed" rather a lot onstage and there was always a man going after him with a shovel, cleaning it up. There was also an entire train in the show. It was petrifying to rehearse: I was a tiny thing amongst a huge cast in a vast theatre, which I adored but was also scared of as I'd been told about all its famous old spooks.

'I never had stage fright, though, thank God. When, occasionally, I'd get a little nervous, the outward sign of it was that I started yawning. Then people around me would be terrified that I would fall asleep and say, "Wake up! Wake up!

You're about to go on!" But I'm generally very confident while playing a character, and less confident when just being myself. A lot of actors are like that. When you're used to being so many different people, you're not always sure who *you* are.'

A couple of years later came the successful revival of the musical *Gypsy*, starring Angela Lansbury. This time Bonnie didn't have to share her role with anyone. After the London run, the producers asked her parents whether they'd allow Bonnie to remain with the company for its US tour. The opportunity was too good to miss. Mrs Langford accompanied Bonnie on the tour of thirteen American cities, followed by a season on Broadway – one year in all.

'Angela Lansbury had a great influence on me during that year. I learned so much from watching her, the way she worked and the way she treated people – work associates and fans. She always had a lovely aura around her. She was (and is) a star, but very human, very approachable. I'll never forget how much it meant to me when she came to my tenth birthday party halfway through the run – the star of the show at a kids' party! I learnt about generosity of spirit from her – an important lesson.

'There were seven kids in the cast and we weren't allowed to neglect our schoolwork. We had a tutor and followed the normal curriculum. The rest of my family came out to see us a few times. One of the best moments of that year was when I got a standing ovation on Broadway, on the last night of the show. There's nothing else like it.'

The run had its (literally) hairy moments, too. 'We had a monkey in the show, called Edith Ann. She was very sweet and I befriended her. She always used to wait for me to come back to my dressing room after my part in the show was over, when I'd feed her a jar of baby food. I was holding her one evening when one of the other kids, playing around, pulled her tail. Edith Ann panicked and bit me. There was no blood but I had these awful teeth marks in my shoulder.

'My mother was very worried, so as soon as the show was

over and I'd taken my curtain calls she rushed me in a taxi to the nearest hospital. By this time it was about eleven at night. The hospital was like a prison, with bars and iron grills everywhere, and the waiting room was full of drunks and vagrants and drug addicts. We hurried up to the desk and my mother, in a real state by now, said to the woman behind the grill, "My child's been bitten by a monkey!"

'We were an incredible sight: this very proper English lady with a little girl in tow wearing full stage make-up. But the woman didn't bat an eyelid. She drawled, "Ok, Ma'am, take a seat over there." I guess she thought we were just another pair of nutcases – you know, in New York anything goes.'

Years later, playing Peter Pan at the Aldwych and flying around the stage in a harness attached to invisible wires, she crashed into the scenery. By the end of the act blood was pouring down her leg. She had to have stitches. But at the following performance the stitches burst. It was a struggle to get through the show. But she'd been a professional since the age of seven, and took such mishaps in her stride.

Actors are a superstitious breed, and most of them keep a talisman of some kind to help them through their perform-ances. For Bonnie, it is a medallion given to her by the nuns at the convent school she attended as a small girl. 'In every show I've been in, I've had it pinned to my costume. This was a problem when I was doing *Cats*, because I wore only a body stocking. So I sewed it into my knickers. When the *Sun* newspaper found out about the good luck charm in my knickers, they made out that it was something saucy. Little did they know it was a medallion of the Virgin Mary given to me by nuns.'

At the outset of her career, her parents opened a building society account for her. Every penny she earned went into it. She was allowed to draw occasionally on the interest, but otherwise the money had to be saved until she grew up and became independent. 'They taught me to have a responsible attitude to money, and they certainly didn't spoil me in any way. For them I was never a "child actor", I was just a child. Of course, I never earned such vast amounts – you don't, in theatre and television work. Not like in the cinema. I was certainly no millionaire, like Macaulay Culkin.

'My family has always been my backbone, my support. In a way, with every show you're in, the cast becomes like a family, you become close to each other. But those families fall apart when the show is over. Your own real family, on the other hand, is always there, providing the fixed point in your life, and normality. And they are honest with you, they're not like the sycophants who come backstage drooling, "You were *won*derful, darling." So you listen to both their praise and their criticism.

'To young girls contemplating a career in show business, I'd say: don't have any illusions. An actor's life has only a small fraction of the glamour people imagine it to have, and a lot more of the hard grind and disappointment; it can be very disheartening. And don't neglect your education. Although I left school at sixteen to work full-time as an actress, I made sure I got my O levels first. It was important to me to know something about the world, to have an understanding of art and literature. How else can you hope to portray characters realistically, and understand the scripts you're given?'

Douglas Adams

'I was keenly aware of the fact that my life was complicated in all sorts of mysterious ways and different to other kids' lives.'

Born in Cambridge on 11 March 1952. Education: Brentwood School, Essex, and St John's College, Cambridge. Career: Radio and television writer, 1974–78; novelist since 1979. Books include: *The Hitch Hiker's Guide to the Galaxy, The Restaurant at the End of the Universe, So Long, and Thanks for All the Fish* and *Dirk Gently's Holistic Detective Agency.*

Douglas lived in Cambridge for only the first six months of his life; then his family moved to London. His father came from a well-off Scots family, but a domestic rupture having left him a poor man, they settled in the East End. When Douglas was five, his parents' vitriolic marriage broke up. That's when he and his sister, together with their mother (a nurse), moved into his grandmother's house in Brentwood, Essex.

'I basically grew up in my grandmother's house. She was a well-known character in the area – the local representative of the RSPCA. The house was always full of an incredible number of dogs and cats, most of whom were either physically or psychologically damaged, because they'd been strays. Any animal nobody else would take, my grandmother would bring home, including badgers, foxes, and even a pigeon which used to crap on everything.

'There was one extraordinary animal, a Pomeranian called Winkle, the most bad-tempered bundle of viciousness you could ever come across. He was an incredibly angry dog – angry at everything and everyone, except for my grandmother, whom he totally adored and loved. He would fiercely guard her and her belongings against all comers. He'd suffered a cerebral haemorrhage, which resulted in his head being permanently tilted to one side, and however loudly and terrifyingly he barked, he couldn't actually bite you – he had no strength in his jaw.

'My grandmother was sometimes involved in training police dogs. And I can remember these huge great dog-handlers that would come over to our house, and there'd be this tiny piece of orange fluff making the most appallingly shrill racket and no one could get near it. Not even the police dog-handlers. It was literally all bark and no bite.

'As a kid I had terrible asthma and hayfever. I sneezed the whole time. My attention span was fifteen seconds, which is about as long as you get between sneezes. In retrospect, I know the problem must have been a result of living in this house crammed with animals, but strangely, nobody thought of that at the time.

'I grew up feeling that animals were what made life difficult – there were always tons of them around, jumping all over the place, making me sneeze and cough. It really put me off pets. If it were possible to have a pet with an "off" switch, I'd consider it.

'My mother worked then as a night nurse at Brentwood District Hospital, so we'd have some money to live on. She slept during the day. So we didn't see much of her. My parents' divorce disturbed me a great deal, but not half as much as their marriage did. Their relationship ranked as one of the major conflicts of the century. They were so antagonistic towards each other, that anything I'd do to please one, was bound to displease the other. The result was that sometimes I felt I couldn't make a move.

'When they divorced, my sister and I became shuttlecock kids, living sometimes with my mother, who was hard up, and sometimes with my father, who remarried and whose second wife was wealthy. So we alternated between being hard up in one family and rather affluent in the other. Of course, whatever happens to you as a kid you just somehow accept. But when you look back, you think – *what*? That was really weird.

'Divorce was very unusual in those days, I didn't really understand what it meant. But I was keenly aware of the fact that my life was complicated in all sorts of mysterious ways and different to other kids' lives. My family has never been very good at talking openly about things. I just had to accept things as they were. There was no one I could confide in, but in any case I wouldn't have been able to articulate my feelings then, because in order to know that you've got a feeling about something, you've got to know what it's like *not* to have that feeling.'

His mother married again, too, to a vet. In time, Douglas acquired a full complement of half-siblings. When he was thirteen his mother and step-father moved to Dorset and Douglas remained at Brentwood as a boarder. By the age of twelve he'd reached his full height of six foot, five inches and looked ludicrous in short trousers. His mother beseeched the headmaster to make an exception in his case and allow him to wear long trousers to school, only to be told he'd have to wait until he entered the senior school – there would be no bending of the rules.

At last he became a senior. Unfortunately, the school had no trousers that fitted him and a pair had to be ordered specially. That took weeks. So, much to his chagrin and everyone else's amusement, for the first few weeks at senior school the towering youth remained in his little shorts.

'My great hobby as a kid was a rather mundane one – making model aeroplanes from kits. I spent a lot of time doing that. I kept them all on top of a large chest of drawers. An early tragedy in my life was when a big mirror which stood behind them fell down and smashed the whole lot. Some sort of light went out of my life at that point.'

Douglas taught himself to play the guitar, and has always had a passion for music. He sang in the school choir. 'One of the perks of being male is that you get to sing treble, then alto, then tenor, then bass, over a period of years.' As a teenager he and a schoolfriend formed a duo, playing together and singing in harmony, performing at school functions and folk clubs. The greatest musical influence on him while he was growing up was the Beatles. 'They kept me in a state of complete and utter amazement, and still do. If I were ever on *Mastermind*, my specialist subject would be the Beatles.

'I was also fascinated by science fiction, which is something that writing *Hitch Hiker* has thoroughly cured me of. I loved comics like *The Eagle*, *Dan Dare* and *Superman*. Films had no influence on me, because I wasn't allowed to see many. And I was permitted to watch very little television. But I absolutely adored and loved English radio comedy –

shows like *Beyond Our Ken*, *The Clitheroe Kid*, and *I'm Sorry I Haven't a Clue* with John Cleese, who was a big inspiration to me. Years later I was in awe of the *Monty Python* TV series. I thought it was the most wonderful thing I'd ever seen. *Python* and the Beatles made an equally big impact on me.

'My fantasy then was to become, like Cleese, a writer/ performer, although I had no real burning ambition to do anything. I used to rack my brains to think of something I'd be good at or interested in. If I'd been born ten or fifteen years later, however, I know without a shadow of a doubt what I would have been: a computer software designer. I'm fascinated by computing, a creative process which is actually very similar to writing.

'The great boon of computers, as far as being a writer is concerned, is that it provides endless scope for putting off the actual business of *writing* something, which, as we all know, is what writers won't do unless and until they absolutely have to. So, instead of sharpening your pencils or cleaning out the fridge or taking a bath – all the usual delaying tactics – you can reconfigure your operating system and move your fonts around.'

As a very young child he had difficulties at school, because he'd been so disturbed by family traumas. He was even tested to see whether he had educational problems. Then, at seven, in his first term at prep school, he astonished everyone by coming top of the class, 'for the first and only time in my entire school career'. Afterwards, he was in the top stream but usually low down the class ('particularly after I discovered girls at sixteen').

As a youngster, just as now, Douglas could write very well, but found it hard work – 'a miserable and distressing job, most of the time'. His English masters at both prep and senior school were talented and inspiring men; both had a major influence on Douglas's understanding and use of language.

'Kids so quickly seize on the eccentricities of teachers.

Later you come to see how lucky you were to be taught by people who were so obsessed with what they did. Bill Barron, my senior school English master, was brilliant. He was impossible in all kinds of ways – an eccentric tyrant, completely mad.

'His obsessions, at least the ones I most remember him for, were with Shakespeare and Keats. Particularly from the way we analysed Keats, I learnt a huge amount about the fundamental way in which words work. Keats' great strength is that his language not only describes, but *is* what it is describing. His words function in the same way as music – they embody the sense of something, rather than stand back from it and talk about it. I wouldn't presume to say that I have this ability myself, but certainly in the best things that I've written, I can see that this influence has been at work.'

Another interesting influence at work in Douglas's writing has been that of his mother. 'She's a wonderful person, although ours is not a particularly easy relationship. She's terribly funny, but she doesn't realize it. She has the most wonderful sense of humour. She tells stories the way that Tommy Cooper does magic tricks; the more of a mess she makes of them, the funnier they become.

'A year ago I recorded a "talking book" version of *Hitch Hiker*. I hadn't read it for a long time, and when I sat down to record it, I was amazed by how much of my mother there was in it. In one line after another I could hear her tone of voice, and the rhythm of her speech. My style owes a great deal to her.'

Douglas claims to have been plagued by worries and self-doubt almost incessantly throughout his life. 'Sometimes I get an acute sense of not really fitting into the world. I'm very tall, which means I have great difficulty in buying clothes. I walk down a high street full of clothes shops and know that none of them are for me. I'm also left-handed. When I go into a shop full of musical instruments, I know that none of them are for me. All sorts of things are a problem when you're left-handed, for example the way that scissors work.

'So I do get this sense of the world having been designed for everyone other than me. I think I've probably always had it. And it must have some effect on me. Then again, because each of us can only ever inhabit his own body, and we have no way of comparing that with the experience of inhabiting someone else's body, we inevitably accept whatever we know as normal. This is one of the things I've been thinking about recently . . . '

Roshan Seth

'We used to emerge from the house each day looking *very* weird indeed.'

Born in Patna, Bihar State, India on 2 April 1942. Education: St Joseph's Convent School; the Doon School; St Stephen's College, Delhi. Career: Actor. Films include: *Juggernaut, Gandhi, My Beautiful Launderette, Passage to India, Little Dorrit, Not Without My Daughter, Mississippi Masala.*

I grew up in a typical upper-middle class milieu in India, but I found that very restricting, so from a young age I was prone to dreaming a lot. To me, the whole ritual of education was pretty meaningless. My head was always miles away, when it should have been on, for example, mathematics. But my Asiatic cunning kept me out of trouble at school. I was like a tortoise: any danger and I'd retract under my shell. There, no one could touch me, I was free to do as I pleased.'

His vivid fantasy life was his only means of escape from the conventional existence which he found so uninspiring. 'Every Sunday afternoon I went with my three brothers and our friends to the cinema in Patna to see an American movie. They fuelled my fantasies. In particular I had a long-running serial in my head, which all took place on a ship – all the big stars used to come and visit me on it: Clark Gable, Humphrey Bogart, John Wayne, Ava Gardner. It never occurred to me then that one could actually make a living from being an actor. I acted in a lot of plays at school, but that was just for fun, like a party game.'

The young Roshan was not only a dreamer, but also rather confused. 'I grew up with a very hazy, mixed-up idea about who I was. In India, it's very important to have a "label", but I never had one. My father, an academic, was Hindu, while my mother was half-English and half-Muslim. They were both anti-religious, although they sent me to schools run by nuns and Jesuit priests.

'I really grew up on the knee of my maternal grandmother, who lived with us in Bihar and was the quintessential Englishwoman. Even her name was utterly Victorian: Alice Maude. She always wore a dress, never a sari. Through her I developed a natural love for the English race. When I moved to London in nineteen sixty-four, it wasn't difficult for me to feel at home.

'She taught me Christian values, the difference between right and wrong, compassion. She was kind to animals – this went against the grain in India, where people treat animals cruelly. Once she saw a bullock-cart driver whipping his bullock, so she snatched the whip out of his hand and thrashed *him* with it.

'She recited bedtime stories to us, and would act out the stories – hers was the first real *theatrical* influence on me. She would cry when she got to the dramatic climax, usually about some poor little orphan in the Dickensian slums, and we'd cry, too. It was always a dramatic performance.

'She could really embarrass us, too. Our hair, like the hair of all Indian children, was dead straight. But she would have it curled into little ringlets before we went off to school, making us look like those Victorian children in old picture-books – it was *absurd*. She also went around with a powder puff. Because India is such a hot country, people sweat and have shiny noses. Grandmother was constantly powdering our noses to take the shine off. So we used to emerge from the house each day looking *very* weird indeed. It all added to the vague mess that I was.'

Adding to Roshan's confusion was the influence of his mother's sister, the beautiful, light-haired Aunt Delicia, who led a wonderfully bohemian existence in the great city of Calcutta. 'She was a freestyle dancer – a kind of Indian Isadora Duncan – who performed with snakes and suchlike. She was totally westernized, a misfit in India. My own home was run like clockwork, all very predictable and ritualistic, so her eccentric and chaotic lifestyle was terribly attractive to me.

'Also, I always preferred the company of our servants to that of our own kind. I would sit with them for hours in the kitchen. They were freer in spirit, more natural, and more interesting to me. My mother, who'd given up her career as principal of a women's college to have a family (and always resented it), never had time for her children, she couldn't show affection to us. But I can still feel the comforting warmth of our *aya*'s arms around me.

'I had a difficult adolescence. There was a lot going on

inside me which I couldn't articulate. I was a rebel, but mine was a *hidden* rebellion, invisible to the outside world. I bottled it up. I was already a young man at college before I found someone who could articulate my feelings for me – the Indian philosopher and mystic, Krishnamurti. It's so important for adolescents with all their inner turmoil to find a spiritual guide.'

It was ironic: Roshan had always been irresistibly drawn to the West – dreaming up scenarios for himself inspired by Hollywood – yet it was this Eastern mystic who helped him come to terms with himself. 'He taught me that it isn't right to conform, to go along with the tide. You must follow your own inner voice. So I finally asked myself – why the hell shouldn't I spend the rest of my life doing what I love and what I want to do, which is to act?

'As a boy I loved possessing odd little things. I'd collect anything. Even the pieces of paper that my father tore up and threw away I would retrieve from the wastepaper bin and keep in a box. Now, of course, I realize that being who you are and what you are, is your most valuable possession.

'My parents used to tell me that it was good to be of mixed background and have the best of both worlds. But I felt one had to be either a goose or a crow. It seemed to me ridiculous to have the top half of a goose and the bottom half of a crow. Now I think it's great. It's made me well-equipped to deal with the cosmopolitan world of international cinema.'

Viviana Durante

'I'm very shy offstage, but when I dance I become
a completely different person.'

Born in Rome, Italy on 8 May 1967. Education: White Lodge
Royal Ballet School. Career: Principal Ballerina, The Royal
Ballet, Covent Garden. *Time Out/01* London Dance Award, 1989;
Dancer of the Year, *Dance & Dancers Magazine*, 1989; *Evening
Standard* Ballet Award, 1989.

iviana started dancing at the age of seven, at a ballet school near to where she lived in Rome. It soon consumed her life. While other little girls were out playing with their friends, she would stay home to practise. She missed a lot of parties so as not to miss a single ballet class. Dancing, even at that age, was much more to her than just the genteel diversion it is to so many young girls.

She was ten when two famous Russian dancers – Galina Samsova and Andrei Prokovsky – who had both defected and were living in London, staged a production of *The Sleeping Beauty* in Rome. As is the custom, they went to the local ballet school to pick out a few children for the minor roles. Viviana, small and delicate, was considered to have the perfect build for the part of the White Cat in the 'Puss in Boots' sequence.

She so impressed the two Russians with her ability that they told her mother she must leave Rome to study ballet at the highest level – either in Moscow or Leningrad, or at the Royal Ballet's renowned White Lodge School in Richmond, on the southern fringe of London. Russia seemed too far away and rather forbidding. So London it was. A couple of months later her whole life changed.

'Like most Italian families, we are very close, so it was a difficult and painful parting – particularly as I was so young. I didn't speak a word of English when I arrived, so I remember being confused much of the time. I hated the unfamiliar food, the damp climate. I was very homesick. It was awful. White Lodge is a beautiful building, a boarding school set in gorgeous surroundings in Richmond Park, but I couldn't appreciate any of that then.

'I remember once, returning from a visit to my family in Rome, feeling a tight knot in my stomach as the taxi drove me up the road to the school, and thinking: I'll never come back again, the next time I go home, I'll *stay* home . . . but I always did come back. The only time I felt all right was

41

when I was dancing. Then I was able to switch off my home-sickness. I loved ballet then, and I love it now.'

Being accepted at White Lodge didn't necessarily mean you would be there for long. At the end of each year the less talented would be filtered out. Viviana had to prove herself constantly. At fourteen she was chosen to be one of four pupils to take part in a television documentary. Its title, *I Really Want to Dance*, was a quote from her, and the pro-gramme's last line.

Only a small proportion of the pupils who successfully complete the course end up in the Royal Ballet. Viviana went straight in at seventeen, about a year younger than usual. Her particular gifts were recognized early.

'Even as a child, I always knew my own mind, I knew what I wanted. This is very important in my dancing, because I hate being *told* what I should be feeling, it's got to be spontaneous and come from inside. I think my Latin blood brings a certain quality to my dancing: warmth and passion. I'm very shy offstage, but when I dance I become a com-pletely different person – I'm temperamental. I just love doing dramatic roles, like Juliet (who is Italian, of course). I can really get inside them.'

At twenty she was promoted to soloist with the company, and soon afterwards her big breakthrough came. It was the classic tale of overnight stardom, like something out of Hollywood.

'We were doing *Swan Lake* one night, and I was dancing in the *corps* as one of the cygnets. Maria Almeida, who was dancing the main part of the Swan Queen, tripped up over some scenery in the wings and injured herself in between the second and third acts. She was in so much pain she couldn't continue the show, and there were still two more acts left.

'All the other Principals had left the theatre and none of the ballerinas there knew the role. The director, Anthony Dowell, came backstage and asked me if I'd like to have a go. I didn't know any of the choreography, but I said, "OK, I'll do it." He and my dance partner tried to show me some of the steps, but there was hardly any time, so I knew I'd have to make most of it up as I went along. To make things worse, the costume was too big for me. I was very scared.

'I came on just at the point when the Swan Queen does the famous thirty-two *fouettés* [turns executed while rapidly whipping the air with a raised leg]. Usually by then a dancer is really tired from the exertions of the first two acts, but I was fresh, so it was easy. Somehow I got through the rest of the ballet (I had to be talked through most of the fourth act by my partner) and I was overwhelmed, I couldn't believe it at the end when the entire audience gave me a standing ovation and threw flowers.'

It was a triumph. The next day her picture was in the newspapers, the public knew her name. It was the first Principal role she had ever danced, and it soon led to others – Cinderella, Juliet, and Princess Aurora in *The Sleeping Beauty*.

'My greatest role model was the late Margot Fonteyn. I was lucky enough to have some coaching from her a few years ago when I played Ondine, the water sprite, a part originally created for her. She showed me some of the movements and everything was so honest about her, there was nothing hidden.

'Antoinette Sibley often takes us for rehearsals, and I absolutely adore her. I can talk to her about anything. I've always been very critical of myself, and she's given me confidence when I've been dissatisfied. And she's always so happy, she makes me smile.

'You can't dance for ever, after a certain age your body can no longer give a hundred per cent. And I would hate to go downhill. But I've no desire to teach or direct. I'm a performer, not a behind-the-scenes person. Acting interests me; perhaps I can do that at a later stage. But for now all I want to do is dance.'

One thing hasn't changed in all the years since she first

arrived, a confused ten-year-old, at White Lodge: she's still homesick. 'In Italy people seem to care more about one another than here, you can always ask your neighbours for help, if you need it. I've been living in the same place in London for five years, and I don't even *know* any of my neighbours.

'I still rely a great deal on my mum and dad, emotionally. They're my best friends. And I go back to Rome whenever I can get away. I've even flown home just for the day.'

She is still petite – all long, slender limbs like a young gazelle. Her delicate physique was what first attracted the attention of Samsova and Prokovsky, the mentors who dramatically altered the course of her life. That accident of birth was her first stroke of luck. But luck can only take you so far, then the rest is up to you.

Prof. Quentin Blake, OBE

'The next thing I knew, I was summoned to the headmaster, who wanted to see the drawings for himself. "Oh no," I thought, "now I'm done for! I'm in the soup!" '

Born in Sidcup, Kent on 16 December 1932. Education: Lamorbey C. of E. Primary School; Chislehurst & Sidcup Grammar School; Downing College, Cambridge; London University Institute of Education. Career: Artist and illustrator. Former teacher of illustration, Royal College of Art; now Visiting Professor. Illustrator of nearly 200 books, including Roald Dahl's *The Twits, The BFG, The Witches, The Enormous Crocodile, Matilda* and *George's Marvellous Medicine*, Michael Rosen's *You Can't Catch Me* and *Quick, Let's Get Out of Here*, Russell Hoban's *How Tom Beat Captain Najork and His Hired Sportsmen*, plus many he wrote himself e.g. *Patrick, Mr Magnolia, Angelo, Mrs Armitage on Wheels, All Join In, Cockatoos.*

uentin Blake grew up in the typically suburban setting of Sidcup. His ordinary middle-class family lived in a house like any other ordinary middle-class family in the neighbourhood. His mum was a housewife, like all the other mums, and his civil servant father, like everyone else's father, took the train to London each morning, briefcase and brolly in hand.

Not the most inspiring background for an artist. Yet by the time he was eight, he had a passion for drawing. 'My brother, being eleven years older than me, was already out of the house, so I was like an only child and had to amuse myself a great deal.' In those days before television had entered people's homes, 'amusement' generally took an active rather than a passive form.

'Neither of my parents were particularly interested in or knew anything about art, so I have no idea where my own interest came from. There wasn't a single art book at home. But we did have a neighbour with a good collection of art books, and when I'd done my homework and didn't know what else to do, I'd pop across the road to look at them. They got used to my sudden appearances.

'I'm ashamed to say I was a boringly *good* child. I inherited my parents' shyness and diffidence. It's a two-sided characteristic – quite nice in a way, but it also holds you back, stops you from really pushing yourself as far as you can go. It's a handicap for an artist, and it took me a long time to overcome it. You need a certain amount of ambition, but that was not instilled in me at home.'

At first his drawings imitated what he saw in comic books and magazines. They were filled with action and movement, but were otherwise unexceptional. Originality came later when, in his early teens, he discovered a fertile theme: the monotony and dullness of suburbia. He produced endless cartoons which poked fun at his surroundings.

'In those days, during the forties, everyone used to go around wearing identical, cheap, ex-navy duffel coats. The people on the streets of Sidcup all looked the same. One of my early cartoons showed a father and his two children, all clad in these duffel coats, arriving at the hospital to see the latest addition to their family. A nurse appears carrying the baby – which is, naturally, wearing a tiny duffel coat.'

From the age of fourteen he regularly sent these witty observations to the humourous magazine *Punch*. 'For two years they were rejected, with slightly encouraging notes. Eventually, when I was sixteen, I was given an appointment to see the art editor. I arrived and was told to sit in the waiting room. I sat and sat, waiting to be seen, for a couple of hours or so, until it was the end of the working day. They thought I was the nephew of someone else who'd come in to see the art editor, and by the time they realized I wasn't just a boy who'd accompanied his aunty, it was too late to see anyone. So I had to go away and return another time. And on that second occasion they did, at long last, buy two of my cartoons. That was really the start of it all.'

This breakthrough marked a crucial turning point: once you are actually paid for your work, and it is published, it can never again be considered a mere 'hobby'. Following the acceptance of those first two drawings, Quentin received a letter saying, 'Congratulations to our youngest contributor', and a cheque for seven guineas. 'It was a tremendous moment. But I had no idea what to do with the cheque, as I didn't have a bank account. So I opened one, and kept a careful account of my (infrequent) earnings.'

His talent earned him a certain renown amongst his schoolmates. And once it very nearly landed him in big trouble. 'Every year our grammar school put on a Shake-speare play, and the headmaster always insisted on being in it, although he usually couldn't manage to learn his part. One year we staged *Julius Caesar*. As you know, in this play the Mark Antony character is a tall, young, athletic, heroic man. And this is the part that the headmaster, who was fat, middle-aged and bald, reserved for himself.

'We hired the costumes from the famous theatrical cos-
tumiers Bermans & Nathans, but the headmaster could
barely get into his leopardskin leotard, and had great difficulty doing up his "Roman" boots. He wore a ginger wig
which was none too secure, and he was also meant to wear
a shaped breastplate with muscles on it, but I can't remember
whether or not he ever managed to get into that.

'I couldn't resist making several drawings of him in his
role. They were the source of great amusement to the boys
at school, who knew enough to keep quiet about it. But
unfortunately the headmaster had a French pupil staying
with him at the time, who foolishly let on about the existence
of my drawings. The next thing I knew, I was summoned to
the headmaster, who wanted to see the drawings for himself.
"Oh no," I thought, "now I'm done for! I'm in the soup!"

'I couldn't see any way out of it, so reluctantly I went to
his office with the two *least* offensive drawings, in which he
was wearing a toga which mercifully concealed some of his
figure. Quaking, I handed him the pictures. He studied them
silently for a while. Then he turned to me and said, "Yes, I
think you've caught something of the essential *energy* of the
man."

'His self-esteem was so impenetrable, he didn't even see
the joke. And I got off scot-free.'

His art teacher at school influenced him greatly, and was
to become a life-long friend. Stanley Simmonds, who was
himself a practising painter, took Quentin's work seriously,
and the two had frequent discussions about art. Quentin also
drew for the school magazine, as well as editing it. All the
stimulation which was lacking at home was provided by
school. Albeit sometimes indirectly.

'When I was eleven or twelve some of my school-friends
and I started a club called the I I I (Idiotic Inventions Incor-
porated). We met at lunchtime and during breaks to tell each
other jokes and other stupid things we'd thought up. We
also kept a book in which we wrote down our "idiotic inven-

tions", none of which I can now remember. One of these friends and I appeared in a Christmas concert at school once, playing a pair of stand-up comics, reciting jokes we'd either made up or pinched.

'You learn a lot at school through lessons, but you can also learn a lot of other, equally important things in these other ways. I once illustrated a book called *How Tom Beat Captain Najork and His Hired Sportsmen*, about a boy who spends all of his time fooling around, yet wins all the games he has to play against the "hired sportsmen" who are paid to do it. He learnt all of his skills by messing about, and became much better at them than the so-called professionals. I think of this story as a kind of allegory about education.'

Although the style for which he has become so well-known as an illustrator has been refined over the years, its essence is the same as it was when he was a schoolboy. 'An artistic style is really a kind of "handwriting", it comes spontaneously from the accents your hand makes. The initial messages come from the brain, but the drawings are on the paper almost before you've had a chance to think about them. You need lots of practice in order to perfect that process, and your individual style.'

The action and movement which animated his drawings as a child are still the most vital elements. 'My pictures are about physical activity, about what somebody is *doing*, they're not still lifes. I identify with what's happening, and almost believe it. Children can recognize that quality, and I think that's why they like my illustrations.'

Jack Straw, MP

'There can't be many people these days, in this country, whose father has been imprisoned for his beliefs rather than for any criminal action.'

Born in Buckhurst Hill, Essex, on 3 August 1946. Education: Oaklands Kindergarten, Staples Road County Primary School, Brentwood (direct grant) School, Leeds University, Inns of Court School of Law. Career: President of the National Union of Students, 1969–71; practising barrister from 1972–74; local councillor, London Borough of Islington, 1971–78; entered full-time politics 1974; Labour MP for Blackburn since 1979; Shadow Education Secretary from 1987–92; Shadow Environment Secretary since 1992.

J ack Straw's parents split up when he was eleven, and from then on he was raised solely by his mother, a teacher at the primary school Jack himself had attended. She came from an Essex family, the Gilbeys, who established a gin business in the mid-nineteenth century. It was set up by two brothers, Walter and Alfred. Walter was very dynamic and was knighted by Queen Victoria; Alfred, Jack's great-great-grandfather, was a drunkard and was thrown out of the firm.

Jack's political ideals are firmly rooted in his family background. He was very close to his grandfather Gilbey, who died when Jack was nine. The old family stories which he handed down to the young boy significantly influenced his views on social issues. 'He was a very bright, but frustrated man who, at the age of thirteen had had to black the boots of the local lord of the manor each day before school. He later became a night mechanic on the buses and an active trade unionist.'

Like Jack himself, his grandfather Gilbey grew up on the edges of Epping Forest, just north-east of London, and was steeped in its lore. He mesmerized his grandson with the story of how, in the 1840s, the agricultural labourers from the villages surrounding the forest took on the local lords of the manor, in order to preserve their age-old right to take wood from the forest and graze their cattle in it. The squires had tried to enclose the forest and keep the commoners out. There were outbreaks of violence over the issue. In the end, a group of villagers based in Loughton, and including Alfred Gilbey (who was a boozer, but a literate one), began a long-running and celebrated legal action against their local squire, and won. The romantic David and Goliath story impressed Jack deeply: he realized that the disadvantaged could take on the powerful and win, if they were determined and organized.

As a schoolboy Jack went to the Essex Record Office and dug out all the documents relating to the case. He saw, scrawled on to the margin of one of the papers, the haughty words written over a century earlier by one John Whitaker Maitland: 'Why should a twenty-five shilling-a-week labourer be allowed to take me, a lord of the manor, to court?'

Jack's father comes from a mining village just outside Barnsley, in Yorkshire. But in 1931, at the age of fourteen, he moved south with his widowed midwife mother – a move from which, according to Jack, he never really recovered. Coming from the north, speaking with a different accent, he was ostracized at his school in Woodford, Essex.

At the start of World War II his father was called up, but he decided to be a conscientious objector. He was gaoled for three months, then put to work on the land with prisoners-of-war. Soon afterwards he met and married Jack's mother, also a pacifist.

'You could perhaps react against the experience of my family, but it's not something you could ignore. There can't be many people these days, in this country, whose father has been imprisoned for his beliefs rather than for any criminal action.' His parents were members of the Labour Party and Jack, too, joined at the age of fourteen.

But being in harmony politically doesn't necessarily mean that people can live together. 'My parents fell out when I was about six or seven. It was absolutely awful. They used to row, in between having more kids. I could never work it out, that combination.'

His parents were strong Congregationalists – members of the United Reform Church – and the family attended church every Sunday in Buckhurst Hill, until the prospect of their divorce loomed ahead. 'Divorce was very unusual in the social circle we moved in, and the minister was anxious to avoid a separation. I remember he came over to discuss it. I was sent upstairs. My mother fell out with him, because she didn't agree with his view that the marriage could be sustained with a bit more prayer.'

This rift ended the Straws' attendance at the minister's

church. But soon afterwards Jack, on a scholarship from Essex County Council, became a boarder at Brentwood School and was attending an Anglican chapel seven days a week. He is still a practising Anglican; religion is a significant factor in his life. 'There is a long and powerful tradition of Christian Socialism in this country.'

Jack's mother had never stopped working as a teacher, and after the break-up of the marriage, she was forced to bring up her five children on her meagre salary, plus a weekly maintenance payment of seventeen shillings and six-pence (87.5 pence) from Jack's insurance clerk father. They lived in a council maisonette. Grandma Gilbey, who lived nearby, looked after the children.

It was a life devoid of luxuries, and Jack felt acutely the contrast between his economic circumstances and that of the majority of the boys at school, who came from much more prosperous families. 'They had cars, televisions, telephones, refrigerators – we had none of those things. It took me two or three years before I even admitted to them that I lived in a council house . . . or that my parents were divorced. It was a matter of self-protection.'

School toughened him up and taught him self-reliance. He was bright, self-confident and highly argumentative. 'We argued politics, or argued about *anything*, morning, noon and night.' (Good training for an MP.) Three weeks before his A levels a boy in his boarding house committed suicide, in the study which they shared. Jack, like many of the other boys, was traumatized by the event, and it badly affected his exam results. He didn't make it to Oxbridge, so he settled instead for a redbrick university – Leeds.

This turned out to be a fortunate decision, and a major turning point in shaping his future. The relaxed, socially-mixed, co-ed atmosphere at university was a refreshing change from the Victorian-style regimentation at Brentwood, with its brutality and dark undertones of sexual hypocrisy. While at Leeds he became President of the NUS, which proved to him that he had 'leadership qualities'. He didn't get a very good degree, because he hadn't worked hard enough. But to show himself that he *was* bright, he afterwards applied himself assiduously to his bar finals, and came third in the entire country.

The next major turning point came in 1974 when Barbara Castle, then Social Services Secretary in the Harold Wilson government, invited the young barrister to be her political adviser. Jack hesitated. 'I was enjoying my work at the Bar and wasn't sure about entering politics full-time. So I sought the advice of my head of chambers (ironically, a Tory MP), who asked me whether, in twenty years' time, I'd rather be a high court judge or in the British Cabinet. I answered, "In the British Cabinet." '

And off he went.

Fatima Whitbread, MBE

'Sport was my saviour. It provided an outlet for all my emotional turmoil . . . '

Born Fatma Vedad in Stoke Newington, London on 3 March 1961. Education: Dilkes Infants and Primary School, Culverhouse Secondary Modern (South Ockendon, Essex), Torells Secondary Modern (Chadwell St Mary, Essex). Career: Javelin thrower. Gold medal, 1979 European Junior Championships, Poland; bronze, 1982 Commonwealth Games, Brisbane; silver, 1983 World Championships, Helsinki; bronze, 1984 Olympics, Los Angeles; silver, 1986 Commonwealth Games, Edinburgh; gold (world record-holder), 1986 European Championships, Stuttgart; gold, 1987 World Championships, Rome; silver, 1988 Olympics, Seoul.

Picture the scene: in a dreary council flat in London a three-month-old baby girl has been abandoned. Hungry, thirsty, ill – she cries for three days before a neighbour finally calls the police. The life of the future world-class athlete, Fatima Whitbread, was saved in the nick of time. Long before competing for Olympic gold, this prolonged and determined cry for survival was her first real trial of strength. And she won.

Her birth was the result of a brief union between two immigrants in London – a Greek-Cypriot barber, and a Turkish-Cypriot woman. It was an unacceptable clash of cultures. When the man rejected the woman, she in turn rejected the baby.

Made a ward of court, she was launched upon an institutionalized childhood – thirteen years of pain, deprivation and frequent ill-treatment. 'By the age of five I was a veteran of children's homes. But being brought up with a lack of love and affection doesn't necessarily mean you don't feel it, or understand it. If anything, it makes it even more important to you and makes you realize what love is really about. Aunty Rae, a "house-mother" at the Essex home I lived in for eight years, was a kind-hearted woman full of Cockney common sense. She involved me in caring for and comforting the smaller kids there. That kept my sanity, helped me to survive. Aunty Rae was a very clever child psychologist. She knew that being needed was a form of being loved. And that was what I craved more than anything.'

She got precious little love from the couple who ran the home – Mr and Mrs Smith. Together they established a reign of terror and cod liver oil. She was a cold, imperious woman with a crooked smile, and his menacing persona earned him the nickname 'Hitler'. Seven children shared a tin of beans for supper. Fatima grew into a fearless rebel.

At school she was a troublemaker: tough, a fighter, with nothing to lose. She was the scourge of teachers, often called in to the headmaster. Neither was she a favourite with the dinner ladies. 'I'd flick peas off the end of my knife, and push into the queue for second helpings. The world wasn't fair, so why should I play by the rules?' More often than not, at the age of ten and eleven, she and her friends would disappear at lunch-time, sneaking into the out-of-bounds library to watch TV and smoke cigarettes: another gesture of defiance.

Her best friend at school was Alma, a black girl. Orphaned at the age of two, she also lived in a children's home. It was only around the corner from Fatima's, but it was a world apart in the way that the kids were treated. 'They wore better clothes than us, and were given enough to eat. The houseparents were kind, and whenever I visited Alma, they'd offer me drinks and biscuits. Alma was happy living there. We grew very close, like sisters. There was quite a lot of racial prejudice against her at our school, which didn't have many black kids. But I always beat up anyone who called her names.'

It was during her last year at junior school that she discovered she was exceptionally good at sport. Called to throw a cricket ball one day, she outthrew everyone at the school, including about a hundred and fifty boys. Being better at something than everyone else gave her a new status at the school. 'It was much later that I realized how close bowling in cricket is to throwing a javelin.' She'd found her natural habitat: the sports field.

'Sport was my saviour. It provided an outlet for all my emotional turmoil, all that aggression which resulted from the unhappy life I was leading. I always felt good when I was running, jumping, throwing, kicking a football. And the more I did all that, the stronger I became. Luckily, the school encouraged competitive sports amongst both girls and boys.'

She became the star of the school netball team. It was a serious business, and the seven team members, together with their earnest young coach, wanted passionately to win the upcoming District Schools Championship. A month before the final, Fatima threw a snowball at a particularly unpopular dinner lady and hit her smack on target ('one of my most successful throws ever'). As a punishment, she was banned from the netball team.

'The entire school demonstrated against the ban, led by the netball team, who refused to play unless I was reinstated. A petition went around the school. Everyone knew they couldn't win the league title without me, so in the end the headmaster relented. Of course we won the championship, and were hailed as heroines.' To the rapturous applause of the entire school at morning assembly, each player received a medal. For Fatima, it was only the first of many.

She'd found her calling – sports – and in so doing, she had found herself. She'd taken the negative force in her life, her intense resentment at having been rejected, and forged it into something positive and superior.

But her anguish was not yet over. At twelve, Fatima was beginning to develop into a young woman, but she still had to share a bedroom in the children's home with several other girls, all younger than her. 'I was well-built for my age. Naturally, it was very embarrassing. In order to avoid the curious stares of the other girls, I'd get dressed under my blankets. I was desperate for my own room, for some privacy.'

But the only available room was given to a thirteen-year-old boy, Sham. Because of his custom of snitching on the other kids, he was the Smiths' undisputed favourite.

Then, out of the blue, the woman who'd given birth to her (Fatima refuses to dignify her with the title 'mother'), and who had, from time to time, put in an unpleasant and disturbing appearance in Fatima's life, claimed to want her back. Fatima duly arrived at the dirty little council flat which the woman shared with two of her other children (from different fathers), and her boozy and repugnant boyfriend. She was surrounded by hostility. 'I realized that the woman only wanted me there because she needed a skivvy. Straight away she ordered me to scrub the filthy kitchen floor, turning me into a Cinderella.'

When one night the woman's boyfriend, drunk as usual, forced himself upon her, Fatima returned, distraught and traumatized, to the children's home. The rape had effectively brought her childhood to an abrupt end. Her despair was complete. 'I felt as though I was coming apart, breaking into separate pieces.' She was helped through the crisis by the caring and reliable Aunty Rae.

She and the Smiths now clashed constantly, and her sense of hopelessness was easily transmuted into rage. The other kids at school abused her at their peril. When one of the nastier bullies, a boy who towered over her, called her a 'bastard' and made sure that everyone in class knew he meant it literally, he had a fight on his hands afterwards in the playground. 'I leapt on him and kept punching him so furiously he didn't know how to react. A teacher pulled us apart.'

As usual, it was sport which saved her. 'That was the lifebelt which stopped me from drowning in my sea of misery.' It was only the country dancing in PE lessons which gave her trouble. 'I couldn't see the point in that stupid dancing, so I usually skipped class and went to the girls' loo to have a cigarette. When I did turn up in class, it was only to disrupt it. I drove the PE teacher crazy.'

Fatima was never interested in the academic side of school. Lessons were something to be dozed through or simply tolerated until the next round of sports, or the next clandestine cigarette. But one lesson in particular made her sit up and listen, and it marked the major turning point in her life. The class was learning about Greek mythology, and Fatima heard the tale of Atalanta. It was like a revelation to her.

Atalanta, too, had been abandoned as a baby, but was raised in the wilderness by a she-bear. She grew up to be the greatest female athlete in ancient Greece. She could run faster than any man, and was a brilliant huntress, killing wild beasts with a javelin. Inspired, Fatima decided to try the javelin, and perhaps add it to her already wide range of athletic skills.

She and Alma belonged to an athletics club called the Thurrock Harriers, which did its training at the Blackshots playing fields. The javelin coach at Blackshots was a strict, no-nonsense woman who had herself once been a javelin thrower on the national team: Margaret Whitbread.

'I fell in love with the javelin. Its flight is the most beautiful, magical thing to see. Mrs Whitbread kept telling me that my parents would have to get me a javelin and the proper boots, if I wanted to have coaching. I couldn't bring myself to tell her that I lived in a children's home. When she found out, she gave me some used boots and a javelin herself.'

Thrilled, she took them back to the children's home and practised throwing in the garden. The javelin went crashing through the french windows of the dining room. The Smiths were livid and forbade her to go anywhere after school for a month, which meant no javelin coaching at Blackshots.

'I had to get a message to Mrs Whitbread to explain the situation, so I secretly sent a letter to her at St Chad's School, where she taught PE. I said I hoped she would let me rejoin her group when my punishment was over, because one day I was going to be the best javelin thrower in the world.'

No empty promise, as it turned out.

The bond grew between them. Margaret, her docker husband, John, and their two small sons took to their hearts the lonely girl who had been desperate all her life for a family of her own. At last, at the age of thirteen, she'd found one. The Whitbreads adopted her, and so her new life began.

'The word "home" suddenly took on a completely different

meaning. I loved being in it so much I didn't want to go out. I skipped school to stay home all day, ironing, baking cakes for my brothers, anything.'

But she couldn't live for long without sports. Soon she had joined 'every team worth playing on' at her new secondary school, Torells. She also stopped smoking. In 1977, aged sixteen, she won in four events at the District Schools Championships, and immediately afterwards won the Southern Counties Championship at Crystal Palace. Knowing by now that she wanted to be a full-time athlete, she left school, dedicating herself wholeheartedly to the javelin, under the guidance of her devoted coach/mother, Margaret Whitbread. At eighteen she entered the record books as the first British woman javelin thrower ever to win the European Junior Championship.

Although the pain of her childhood has left its scars, and she still has occasional nightmares, Fatima can see a certain benefit in those early hardships. 'The children's home I grew up in wasn't a happy one, but we had a strict routine which instilled discipline in us. You had to do daily chores in order to earn your pocket money – fold your clothes away, lay the table, wash up, wipe up, clean the floor. As a child it all seemed a real grind, but it made me realize very early on that life has its routine, its discipline – essential elements in an athlete's life.

'And at my first children's home, in Hertfordshire, where we were all aged under five, we had to walk to the nearest village and back each day, in all weathers – four miles in all. It was arduous and exhausting for us, but I'm sure that it gave me valuable early experience of endurance training!'

It distresses her to think of the rejected children of the world, growing up today facing the same agonies which she endured. But she has words of encouragement for them. 'In life, you never know what's just around the corner. It's important to stay strong and keep up your faith, so that when your chance comes to make something of your life, you can grab it.'

Perhaps the adolescent Fatima, imprisoned by her despair, saw the javelin – which can be made to soar magnificently through the air – as the perfect symbol of freedom. In her life, just as in the myth of Atalanta, it was the javelin which slew the 'wild beasts'.

According to the myth, when Atalanta's fame as an athlete had spread throughout Greece, the father who'd abandoned her as a baby proudly stepped forth to reclaim her as his long-lost daughter. And in an extraordinary example of life imitating mythology, the man who had fathered Fatima also appeared one day after she had begun to make a name for herself. He told her that he was now very rich and would like to sponsor her.

'I refused to take his money. And I never saw him again.'

Rabbi Julia Neuberger

'The police rode towards us and in the confusion I was kicked by a horse and was very badly bruised. But it didn't put me off demonstrations.'

Born Julia Schwab in Hampstead, London on 27 February 1950. Education: South Hampstead High School for Girls; Newnham College, Cambridge; Leo Baeck College, London. Career: Rabbi, South London Liberal Synagogue, 1977–1989. Social campaigner.

Julia's early years were suffused with the liberal, intellectual atmosphere of the north London suburb of Hampstead. In the thirties and forties Jewish refugees from central Europe settled in the area, enriching its already cosmopolitan character. She had a close relationship with the paternal grandmother who'd worked arduously before and during the war to help Jews escape from the Nazis.

'My father was a civil servant, with a strong work ethic which I've inherited. Times were hard during my early childhood; we lived in a rented flat without central heating. My father sweated blood to pay my school fees – he only earned about three hundred and fifty pounds a year, and I remember he played the football pools to try to supplement the family income.

'When my mother was pregnant with me she had to leave her job at Marks & Spencer, and afterwards worked for an organization which helped Holocaust survivors. She worked throughout my childhood, with the aid of a series of mother's helps and au pairs, almost all from Germany.

'I was an only child, growing up in the midst of German Jewish *émigrés*, on both sides of the family – grandparents, great-aunts, etc. I was always aware of what it meant to be a Jew, both by religion and by identity. We were observant, but not Orthodox; I was brought up in the Reform tradition.'

Her first and long-lasting ambition was to be an archaeologist. The Keeper of Western Asiatic Antiquities at the British Museum was a good friend of her father's, and he'd allow her to wander through the galleries on weekends, when it was closed to the public. 'He introduced me to the subject as a much more *living* thing than it was at school. From the age of nine or ten I was fascinated by the archaeology of Iraq (known as Babylonia in ancient times), and I eventually went to Cambridge to study precisely this: it's called Assyriology.'

Her grandmother had perhaps the greatest influence on

her while she was growing up. 'She was a formidable lady, with a tremendous social conscience, and a very good grandmother. From early childhood I discussed all kinds of issues with her, we argued about Judaism (unlike me she was Orthodox) and about ideas of social responsibility. She lived nearby in West Hampstead, and I often went to visit her after school. I loved being with her.'

Something of a swot, Julia was also in many ways the typical sixties raver – there was no shortage of boyfriends, parties and dances during her teenage years. 'Partly because I was an only child, friends have always mattered hugely to me. And I tried to be fashionable. I ironed my hair, like most other girls (my mother says it still smells singed). I was into clothes, although I was hopeless at them. There was a great craze for those open-toed white boots with a slit on the side and twist of leather at the top, which I wore during one terribly cold winter and got chilblains on both big toes as a result. Another time I wore a dress I'd made myself to a party – a trendy bright orange shift – which came completely unravelled while I was dancing. Most embarrassing.

'I was always rather overweight and spent a lot of time trying out different diets, none of which worked. At sixteen I became interested in cooking and made things like risottos and pasta dishes – which my mother didn't do. She disliked such "mucked-up food", as she put it, and preferred plain joints, but I could never bear great lumps of meat. And to my fury she always piled more on my plate even before I'd finished what was already on it . . . a real "Jewish mother". That's probably why I was overweight in the first place.'

Julia has always been amazingly active. As a child she collected stamps, read voraciously, attended operas, played the violin and produced mountains of cut-out paper dolls (most of which are now housed in the Bethnal Green Museum of Childhood). And true to her left-wing

Hampstead milieu, from an early age she was actively involved in the social issues of the day. She's a veteran of many a sixties left-wing demonstration.

'I was involved in the nuclear disarmament marches, when I was about fourteen (I remember always being hungry on them). I campaigned for Ben Whitaker, who became the Labour MP for Hampstead. Then at seventeen I attended the big demo against the Vietnam War at the American Embassy. We marched along Oxford Street and when we got to Grosvenor Square we were met by mounted policemen. The police rode towards us and in the confusion I was kicked by a horse and was very badly bruised – I was lucky my thighbone wasn't broken. But it didn't put me off demonstrations.

'Social injustices have always appalled me – racist attitudes, urban housing problems – and I've always been outspoken. It never got me into trouble, because I was rather polite, which is how one gets away with it, I think. My parents certainly encouraged me to be outspoken; we had heated political debates. Also, I used to get angry at the "marxist-speak" of a lot of people involved in our causes. They'd go on learnedly about "the dialectic of materialism" and when I asked them what it meant, they couldn't tell me.

'If there's one thing I regret terribly it's that I was never involved in any serious physical activity. My parents never took any exercise, and they didn't encourage me to, either – a major fault of my upbringing. I was a complete wally at school team sports, but I could have done something else – sailing or swimming or horse-riding. Being *intellectual* doesn't mean you should neglect the physical side of things.'

It wasn't until her fourth year at Cambridge University that she decided to become not an archaeologist, but a rabbi. In the late sixties and early seventies Jews were not allowed into Iraq. The alternative would have been neighbouring Turkey, but British archaeologists were unpopular there at the time, because one of them was supposed to have stolen finds from a site. 'As both a Jew and a Brit, I didn't seem to have a great future in Ancient Near Eastern archaeology (except in Israel where they've got more archaeologists than they know what to do with).

'I'd been studying Hebrew as my subsidiary subject, and so I decided to change it to my main subject. Then one of my tutors suggested that I might become a rabbi. At first I thought it was a ridiculous idea, but after a while it began to interest me. So he arranged for me to do the four-year rabbinical course at Leo Baeck College.

'Rabbis are essentially scholars and teachers, and I became involved in teaching both youngsters and adults in my congregation about the parallels between Hebrew biblical stories and Babylonian literature, and showing them common sources. One of the things a rabbi does, or ought to do, is to place the origins of Judaism in their historical context.'

She became the second woman rabbi in Britain, and the first anywhere in the world to have her own congregation. But she has never ceased her fervent campaigning for civil liberties and human rights.

'My involvement in the Campaign Against Racial Discrimination as a teenager taught me to work together with people of many races and political views, and growing up amongst refugees has enabled me to identify with refugees of all kinds in this country. These are the critical lessons of my early years.

'Racial and religious intolerance are central issues for me. Ironically, it's precisely because I'm a religious Jew that I have such respect for Muslims and the serious ideas within Islam; I can understand the thinking. There's a lot more which links the two religions than divides them. Naturally, I don't agree with fundamentalists, who discriminate against women, but neither do I agree with fundamentalist Jews or the Southern Baptists in the US, who do the same.'

Her Hampstead upbringing and the odd kick from a policeman's horse had clearly turned Julia into a model of Political Correctness long before that trendy term was ever coined.

Timmy Mallett

'If I was chatting up a girl at a party, someone would shout "Watch him – he's the vicar's son!" As if *I* shouldn't be having any fun. *Bleugh*!'

Born in Marple, Cheshire on 18 October 1955. Education: Rose Hill County Primary School, Marple; Earnseat Prep School, Cumbria; Hyde County Grammar School for Boys, Manchester; Warwick University. Career: Radio disc jockey; children's television presenter – shows include: *Wacaday*, *Wide Awake Club* and *Utterly Brilliant*.

immy grew up in the north of England. His home life was happy and harmonious. He has two older brothers, one of whom, Martin, has Down's Syndrome. 'I spent a lot of time with Martin, who is two years older than me, because he always played the games I chose. And I used to win, which was fun. I also learnt early on that it was important that I let Martin win sometimes, otherwise he'd get fed up and refuse to play.

'We were cub scouts together. I remember one dreadful night when we were on our way to a cubs meeting and these bigger boys stopped us and started taking the mickey. I had to try to fight them off; it was really scary. In the end we did a runner. When we arrived at cubs Martin was in tears. So the older scouts went out and duffed up the street lads who'd attacked us, which was great. Martin was walked home that night and made a big fuss of and turned into a kind of hero.

'Later, in our early teens, we went to the pictures together a lot. When we got home he'd explain the film we'd seen, and as he couldn't speak properly, he'd act them out. He was brilliant at it. He was very observant and picked up funny little details that I missed. Without his disability he could have been a great actor. I think I developed a better eye for detail by watching him.

'My father was in advertising, a pretty boring sort of job, I think. Then suddenly, when I was about ten, he jacked all that in to become a clergyman – an extraordinary and courageous thing to do. So he spent a couple of years studying theology. We had no money coming in during that time, so things were very tight, especially as I'd just started boarding at Earnseat School. Our financial problem was solved by some distant member of the family dropping dead and leaving us money. Thank heaven for wills.

'My father took his first parish as a curate in Hyde, Manchester, where I went to grammar school. With a vicar as a father, you get used to the house being constantly full of parishioners wanting to talk about something or another, and the phone ringing just as you're about to sit down to a meal. The place was always buzzing.

'Also, we acquired a certain standing in the community. A vicar, like a policeman or a judge, is a figure of respect, and this rubs off on the other members of his family. As I got to my teens and wanted to be my own person, suddenly I was labelled "the vicar's son" and put on to this different platform. I found it difficult to live with and rebelled against it. People would point to me and say, "That's the vicar's son over there". I didn't like it at all. If I was chatting up a girl at a party, someone would shout "Watch him – he's the vicar's son!" As if *I* shouldn't be having any fun. *Bleugh*!

'But my Dad and I had a very good relationship. When I was doing my A levels, we used to have interesting conversations about his sermons. We talked about Thomas Cranmer and the Reformation, things like that. I'd say "Well, what do you think about the great schism?" or "The Thirty Years' War, Dad – when are you going to put *that* into a sermon?" and he'd say, "Oh, don't start that again . . . "

'I used to go in for a lot of school debates. One of the debates we were set was, "This house does not believe that there are fairies at the bottom of the garden." I wondered how I was going to tackle it. I took some notes and worked out a few rational arguments, but I didn't have a conclusion, so I asked my Dad over tea whether he had any suggestions. He pondered for a moment, then gave me the line with which I ended my speech and won the debate: "Fairies at the bottom of the garden? Fairies my arse!" The audience loved it, they all stomped and cheered like crazy. Good on my dad, the Vicar.'

Timmy claims to have been utterly brilliant at school, but I don't think we have to take that literally. Nevertheless, he did pretty well. And he particularly enjoyed his four years at boarding school, between the ages of nine and thirteen. 'I learnt a lot there about standing on my own two feet. I liked the school and the people and what I was being taught, and I loved its beautiful location, overlooking the estuary and with distant views of the mountains of the Lake District.'

Timmy's greatest adolescent pastime was ringing church bells – called campanology. 'It got you out and about. You went to churches in different towns; there'd always be a pretty girl there – that was quite important. There was absolutely no point in going back to a place that didn't have a pretty girl. I'd either go on a Sunday or on practice night. I knew what the bells were like in all the neighbouring churches, the ring of eight, ring of ten – with the really big, heavy bells – and I knew which churches had dark, nasty bell towers, and which were the naff ones with only one bell. Who'd go to a church with only one bell? If you get really good at bell-ringing, they let you do a peal, in which you ring every combination of eight bells: it lasts for about three hours. I finally packed it in at seventeen, when I became too busy with academic work.'

His worst teenage anxiety was caused by his height, or lack of it. (These days he is 5 foot 4 inches.) 'I was playing rugby one day for school, and when I got hold of the ball and was about to score a try, the sports master, thinking it was terribly funny, picked me up and ran me and the ball down to the other end of the pitch. Everybody loved it. And I just felt *awful* – I wanted the ground to open up and swallow me.

'I was too small to get the girls I really fancied. I was always falling madly in love with some girl who'd never even *see* me. And then when a girl happened to fall in love with *me*, I'd think "Ugh! I don't like her! No!" And I'd do a runner. Being a teenager is terrible. All those worries. Everybody's got a hang-up: your nose is too big or your hair isn't right . . . sometimes you want to be taken seriously, sometimes you want to be indulged as a child. It's the same for everyone.'

The idea of going into radio as a career began to bubble away in Timmy's mind from the age of about fifteen. He'd always adored the world of pop charts and DJs, and was enormously attracted to the 'magic' of sitting in a studio and talking to millions of people. He admits that the fame appealed to him, too. Rolf Harris, who 'was and is brilliant', was an important influence on him, as one of the earliest multi-media personalities in children's entertainment.

By the time he went to Warwick University to study history, Timmy had decided that his future lay in broadcasting. But he liked history as a subject, and didn't mind postponing his working life for another three years. 'I would strongly recommend pursuing subjects at school and college that you enjoy and are interested in, not subjects that someone has told you would be better in terms of a career structure. That's just pandering to the system, isn't it? You have to find your own way, and if the system doesn't support what you want to do, don't feel obliged to be part of it.'

While at Warwick he worked as a DJ for the campus radio station, loved it and took to it so naturally that his tutor told him it was obvious he'd be doing it one day as a full-time job. (He used to get into trouble for talking too much; now it became a positive asset.) The public personality for which the nation's kids know him today has evolved from those early years on campus radio, and that stint led to his first professional job on leaving university – at BBC Radio Oxford. Radio finally led to television, in 1986.

He's still interested in history, which is 'full of good stories', and often injects historical themes into his TV programmes, for example his *Wacaday* filming reports from around the world. 'Frederick the Great of Prussia used to keep an army of giants. That's of no use in an essay, but it's really good if you want to dress up in an army uniform and put on stilts and go around interviewing people to see if they're tall enough for your army – actually at the Charlottenburg Palace in Berlin. That was *great*!'

Perhaps the reason he's been so successful in broadcasting is that he's always found it such fun. And fun – lots of whacky, zany fun – is the keynote in all his work. 'I think fun is really, really important. It develops you, it makes you more of an all-round person, to have lots of fun and laughter in your life. It keeps you sane. Otherwise you'd go nuts with worrying about things. I also believe in a bit of mischief. If I've learnt one lesson in life it's that when you're told off for getting into mischief, you should say "I'm terribly, terribly sorry. I'll never do it again", then carry on exactly as before . . . ha!'

What does the Revd Mallett think of his son's nutty public persona, the Timmy who's on the telly sticking his tongue out and making nonsense noises, hitting people over the head with a mallet and generally advocating mischievousness?

'My father's retired now, but still does the odd sermon here and there. It's all a bit embarrassing, people knocking on his door to ask about me: "Hey, are you really . . . ?" and he moans, "Oh my God, why doesn't he have a normal job? Why isn't he *normal*?" '

It's perfectly understandable. After all, the Reverend still has a certain respectable position to uphold in the community. And if life is tough when you're labelled 'the vicar's son', how on earth do you cope with being known as 'Timmy Mallett's dad'?

Sir Robin Day

'I led a rebellion in my final year at the school. It was all to do with being deprived of our rations of Spam . . . '

Born in Hampstead Garden Suburb, London, on 24 October 1923. Education: Henrietta Barnett kindergarten; The Crypt Grammar School, Gloucester; Brentwood School, Essex; Bembridge School, Isle of Wight; St Edmund Hall, Oxford University. Career: Barrister from 1952–53. Political journalist, television and radio interviewer and presenter since 1955. Programmes include: *Panorama*, *World at One*, *Question Time*.

hen I was at kindergarten I once tripped up one of the mistresses with a hockey stick. Heaven knows where I got a hockey stick from. Luckily, she escaped serious injury. That was the first (but not the last) time that my sense of humour got me into hot water.

'The most painful memory of my early boyhood is of being caned by the headmaster for creating a disturbance during morning assembly. I got three strokes on the palm of my hand. It happened on my tenth birthday. But I carried on being a bumptious, unruly, talkative boy – a nuisance most of the time.'

Some of the famous politicians who he was later to confront as Britain's first and foremost political interviewer on television might also have been tempted to cane his palms. The 'grand inquisitor', as he was called, liked asking tough, provocative questions. But in the end he was rewarded for pioneering political journalism on TV – he became the first 'knight of the box'.

How did he come by his bold, probing style?

'My father had the greatest influence on me. He was an electrical engineer and a civil servant, but with a passion for politics and parliamentary institutions. I was brought up to love political argument. When I was nine he took me to see his hero, Winston Churchill, give a speech at a fête in Gloucestershire. It was raining and we were inside a marquee, but the marquee began to leak. A forest of umbrellas went up and my father interrupted the speech by shouting, "Put those umbrellas down – we can't see Mr Churchill!" I was petrified that he'd be arrested by the police for creating a disturbance. But the umbrellas went down. We got damp, but had a good view of Churchill.

'And I absorbed a healthy irreverence for people in important positions from the headmaster of Bembridge School, where I boarded from the age of fourteen. J. H. Whitehouse was unconventional, a man of originality and vision. He introduced into the curriculum weekly sessions in civics and current affairs, in which each boy would have to hold forth on a particular topical subject and answer questions about it. Whitehouse would often come back from a visit to London, where he'd attended a debate in the House of Commons, and describe some eminent politician as "crackbrained" a "stupid fool" or a "lunatic". That was most refreshing to us schoolboys.'

But the headmaster was to find that a 'healthy irreverence for people in important positions' could be turned against him, too.

'I led a rebellion in my final year at the school. It was all to do with being deprived of our rations of Spam, a delicious tinned meat from America. (This was during the war, and our food rations were precious to us.) The school was storing many large tins of Spam for emergencies, but those of us who were leaving at the end of term didn't see why *our* Spam, supplied on *our* ration points, should be saved for others. As head boy I went to the headmaster's study to claim our rights. He was furious and threatened to expel me. I told him I was leaving in a fortnight anyway. My rational arguments must have persuaded him, in the end, because we got our Spam the next day.

'We had lots of books at home and as a young boy I was always encouraged to read. I was given the collected stories of Sherlock Holmes for my thirteenth birthday. One of the stories, called *The Speckled Band*, disturbed me so much I couldn't sleep that night. It was terrifying, especially the part in which the snake – trained by Dr Grimesby Roylott, late of India – crawls down the bell-pull in the bedroom. I still have that same book, and it's still one of my favourites.

'I adored cricket. My heroes were Wally Hammond, and Len Hutton, whom I saw making his record innings in 1938 at the Oval – three hundred and sixty-four caught Hassett bowled O'Reilly! My favourite possession in those days was a cricket bat signed by a couple of the well-known cricketers. I used to take it to bed with me, I was so attached to it, though I wasn't much of a player myself. I was never very good at any sport (partly because I wore glasses from the age of fourteen), which is something I've always regretted.

'I also bitterly regret not learning to play a musical instrument. I'd particularly have loved to play the jazz piano. As it is, the height of my musical achievement has been to sing 'Underneath the Arches' on the *Des O'Connor Show* a few years ago. I was very interested to see that Des couldn't play the piano, either.

'As a boy I liked making things. I was good at woodwork. I remember, shortly before my sixteenth birthday, I was in the garden making a model boat when Neville Chamberlain's speech declaring war on Germany came on over the wireless. I later listened to Churchill's historic broadcasts on my bedside headphones at school. I had, of course, been expecting war, having already tried on gas masks along with the other boys at school. We all knew that soon enough we'd join one of the fighting services.' (Robin enlisted in the army on leaving school in the summer of 1942, but, to his disappointment, saw no action during the war.)

'The first public event I recall was the abdication of Edward VIII in nineteen thirty-six. I was thirteen. I'd been fascinated by the drama of the King who'd rather give up the throne than Mrs Simpson, the woman he loved. I followed it in detail, keeping a scrapbook of newspaper cuttings. I became an expert on the whole affair, and even memorized pointless information, such as the King's seven Christian names, which I could rattle off in order to anyone who cared to listen, and I still can: Edward Albert Christian George Andrew Patrick David.'

When young Robin, temporarily under the influence of a bible-class leader, announced that he wished to become a missionary in the jungle, his sensible, practical mother didn't object. She merely pointed out that he'd probably get yellow fever. He changed his mind.

As he left school and entered the army, he had a vague

idea of one day becoming a teacher. But when the war was over he chose law instead, qualifying as a barrister. After practising for only one year, he decided he had neither enough money nor the required ability. Before long he'd found his way into broadcasting as a political journalist. 'I've always been addicted to politics.'

Before 1955 Robin's life had been completely untouched by television. He'd hardly ever seen a TV set. He'd never owned one or lived in a house which had one. But since 1955, when he joined ITV, his entire life has been dominated by it. It put him, as he says, 'into orbit' – he and his characteristic bow-tie. ('That's another thing I picked up from my father.')

The most important lesson of his life, and he learnt it early on, is that one must never take things at face value. 'Pay attention to what people say, but at the same time question it and test it against your own thoughts – that's the way to acquire strength of mind.' His advice to kids is that they should get into the habit of doing what he himself became famous for – asking critical questions.

'There are tremendous pressures of fashion and uniformity among the young, which depress me greatly. When I was young, the important thing was to be different from everybody; now the important thing is to be exactly the same. Kids all want the same hairstyle, the same clothes. They all love Arnold Schwarzenegger or Madonna. They don't have the originality or initiative to say "that's a bore". I can't remember, as a youngster, ever being obsessed with fashions or personalities. But perhaps I don't look back accurately.'

Andrew Sachs

'So I said, "But *I* like Hitler – I love him! Didn't you and I go around together collecting milk-bottle tops for the war effort?" '

Born in Berlin, Germany, on 7 April 1930. Education: Zinnowald Schule and Pfalzburgerstrasse Schule, Berlin; Hatch End primary school, Haverstock Hill primary school, Harvist Road junior school, William Ellis grammar school, London. Career: Stage, television and film actor; playwright.

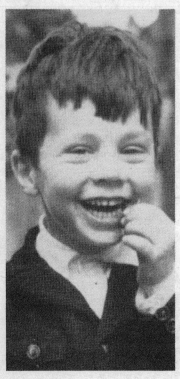

he actor who played the most famous Spaniard on British television, the bumbling waiter Manuel in the *Fawlty Towers* comedy series, is not Spanish at all, but was born in Germany shortly before Hitler came to power.

'My father came from a wealthy Jewish banking family which had lost a fortune during the inflation of the nineteen twenties. (They were reduced to having only four servants – a real hardship!) I think he had an allowance, which gave us a comfortable existence, so although he'd qualified as a lawyer, he never really had a proper job, he wasn't a career man. He was very patriotic, and it appalled him that the Nazis should want to throw him out – after all, he'd won the Iron Cross in the First World War.

'My mother came from a mixed background: part North German Lutheran (they're rather dour, humourless people up there; flat, like the landscape), and on her father's side, peasant stock from the Tyrolean Alps – hence we've all got short, stubby legs in my family, good for climbing mountains. My maternal grandfather was a novelist, very difficult and eccentric, mad really. He'd been ill and was paralysed, and suffered from an ancient wound received during a duel, which made the bones keep coming out of his ears.'

Even a small boy such as Andrew soon learned the harsh lessons of Hitler's new regime of terror. The persecution of the Jews became a common, everyday occurrence on the streets of Berlin. 'The Nazis used to go around painting a large yellow "J" on the windows of Jewish-owned shops, and you were then supposed to boycott them. I remember there was a shop right next to my school, and when I passed it with a group of friends one day we saw the "J" on its window. But the owner had put a notice out saying, "This shop is not owned by Jews." One of my friends remarked sarcastically, "Ah! The first Aryan Jew in history!"

'On another occasion I saw a boy not much older than me, in the uniform of the Hitler Youth, hit an old Jewish man on the street. (This was quite an acceptable thing.) But, to his surprise, the old man picked him up and gave him a spanking right then and there.

'Once my mother nearly got into a lot of trouble. She found herself in a crowd of people watching a fire. "What's going on here?" she asked, and someone told her. "They're burning the synagogue down – serves them right." So she got very angry and started arguing with the crowd. A man pulled her aside and advised her, for her own safety, not to linger.

'My best friend, Ralph, a schoolmate of mine, told me one day that he wasn't allowed to play with me anymore. I asked him why. He said, "Because your father's Jewish. The Jews don't like Hitler very much, and that's not very nice of them." So I said, "But *I* like Hitler – I love him! Didn't you and I go around together collecting milk-bottle tops for the war effort?" But it didn't do any good. Actually, he was just as puzzled by the whole thing as I was. I just thought: all right, fine. And I accepted it. I can't say I suffered or took it to heart, really. I was under the protective umbrella of my parents.'

Andrew was eight when, in the autumn of 1938, events came to a head for the Sachs family, with his father's arrest. 'We'd been to the circus that afternoon and afterwards felt like having a snack, so we went to a cafe across the road from our flat. There was a sign at the door saying something typically absurd like, "No Jews or dogs allowed", and my father hesitated about going in. But my mother would have none of it. "Of course we'll go in if we want – it's *our* country. We'll show them." So we sat down at a table.

'A little later a black-uniformed policeman came in, stood with his hands on his hips and looked around, then made straight for our table. My father was carrying a cutting of a newspaper article criticizing the regime; it was found, and he was taken away. He was released a few days later, but the shock was enough to make him realize that we would have to leave Germany right away. He spoke good English, and had some contacts here, so London was the obvious choice of refuge. He came first, the rest of us – my mother, brother, sister and I – arrived three months later.

'We couldn't take our money with us, but we managed to take some possessions – a few pieces of our massive German furniture, which barely fit into the little semi-detached house we rented in the north London suburb of Hatch End. But I always had clothes to wear, food to eat, there was love in the family – so this upheaval was no problem to me. I think I inherited my mother's resilience.'

The first culture shock took place on the very first morning that Andrew and his family arrived in England. They were having breakfast in a Southampton hotel when something strange appeared on the table. Shredded wheat. 'We all just stared at the little heaps of hay, wondering how on earth the English could eat this stuff meant for horses. Anyway, we ate it, with some difficulty. It never occurred to us to put milk on it.'

A half-year later, the Second World War broke out. Being German then didn't make you particularly popular at Hatch End Primary School. 'Some of the kids called me names: *dirty German Jewish pig*, things like that. But I shrugged it off; that was just part of school. It was no worse than being picked on for being fat or short-sighted. It doesn't really matter what happens on the *outside*, but how you react to things. I wasn't insensitive, but you can overdo being sensitive to your own feelings. It's better to be sensitive to other people's feelings.'

His father was fifty-three years old when the family came to England, not an easy age at which to begin an entirely new way of life. He turned into a hard-working insurance broker, earning seven pounds a week. In the evenings, during the war, he was a fire-watcher. Andrew saw very little of him. In 1944 he died of stomach cancer, leaving his widow to cope on her own. A well-educated, capable woman who'd been a librarian in Germany, she became an expert in

Swedish massage, then worked as a paid companion to elderly ladies and gentlemen. 'She had some wonderful stories to tell about the rich old dears.

'I was fourteen when my father died, and after that I went downhill at school. I'd always had an ambition of one sort or another. I'd wanted to be an artist, a sculptor, an astronomer, an explorer – it changed every week. When I was sixteen I left school announcing that I was going to be an actor . . . to be more precise, I wanted to be a *famous film star*, to sign autographs, go to premiers, have my picture in the movie magazines. I thought it couldn't be that difficult because even dogs become film stars – look at Lassie.

'As the youngest, I was my mother's favourite child, she'd always spoilt me rotten. I easily persuaded her to pay for my tuition at drama school. But after a couple of terms of ballet and movement and diction, I thought – this is useless, I'm not any nearer to being a film star. Where are all the talent scouts from Hollywood? Anyway, my mother couldn't really afford the seventeen guineas a term. So I got a job at four pounds a week as assistant stage manager in rep at Bexhill-on-Sea, where I was given occasional small parts to play.

'I sent my mother money each week; it was quite possible to save on four pounds. I was proud to be helping her out financially, as my brother and sister were doing. But otherwise I wasn't very happy there. *Still* the Hollywood talent scouts didn't discover me! I wasn't impatient, I just felt that seven weeks was long enough to wait.

'In nineteen forty-nine the Army caught up with me – conscription. They wanted to "make a man" of me, but instead they made me an office clerk. So I kept a low profile for two years, considering myself too *precious* to be a soldier. I was an *artist*, I couldn't drive around in tanks.'

At last, after his two years in the Army, he buckled down to learning seriously the craft of acting at the repertory theatre in Worthing, where he came under the good influence of disciplined, professional theatre people. His teenage dreams of film stardom faded into the background as he, too, acquired expertise, discipline and professionalism. His work in the theatre led to opportunities in radio, television and films. He began to write plays when he realized that he was capable of creating better parts than many of those he was offered.

In 1975 John Cleese offered him the role of Manuel. The two series – twelve episodes in all – took him only three months to make. Yet they were the most pivotal three months in a career spanning more than four decades. The part made his name.

'People feel sorry for Manuel. They say, "Ahh, poor chap, always getting clouted by Basil Fawlty." *I* certainly don't see him like that. I see him as an admirable, even heroic man: he's deeply loyal, doesn't harbour resentments, he's conscientious, committed to his job, generous . . . the only thing he lacks is intelligence. But I think intelligence can be overrated, compared to these other virtues.'

He believes that the special circumstances of his life have fostered his comic skills. 'Being uprooted from one culture to another was a major formative influence. Since then I've always felt a bit detached about life – like an outsider looking in, and the world of comedy *requires* that kind of detachment. You must be an observer, able to stand outside things, even outside yourself. In tragedy you feel the pain of the man slipping on the banana skin; in comedy you see the absurdity of it.

'After we came to England I no longer felt German, yet I didn't feel English, either. I was neither Jewish nor completely Christian. I'm even ambidextrous – born left-handed but trained to write with my right. All these ambiguities have made me inclined to "sit on the fence", to remain nonpartisan. I've never joined a political party, for example: I can see both sides of every issue.

'The Germans are always accused of not having much humour, they see everything in black and white – *ziss is correct, und ziss is not correct!* – very priggish, and I think I was like that, too. My outlook would have been very different had I remained in Germany. I'm glad I've been living in the looser, more tolerant atmosphere of England, even though it took me a very long time – I think I was thirty-five or forty – before I really began to feel that I belonged here.'

Rt Hon. Christopher Chataway

'If as a young child you're brought up with the sights and sounds and smells of Khartoum, you don't think that the world has always got to be like Woking.'

Born in Chelsea, London, on 31 January 1931. Education: Forres Preparatory, Swanage; Sherborne School; Magdalen College, Oxford. Career: Olympic runner in 1952 (Helsinki) and 1956 (Melbourne); was pacer for Roger Bannister, helping him to break the four-minute mile in 1954; broke 5000 metre world record in London–Moscow match, 1954. Television newscaster and reporter, 1955–59, first for ITN, afterwards for the BBC. Conservative MP for Lewisham North 1959–66 and Chichester 1969–74; junior education minister under Macmillan; Minister of Posts and Telecommunications, Minister for Industry under Heath. Chairman of Civil Aviation Authority, and of Crown Communications.

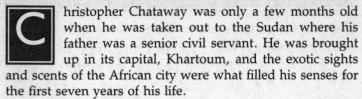 hristopher Chataway was only a few months old when he was taken out to the Sudan where his father was a senior civil servant. He was brought up in its capital, Khartoum, and the exotic sights and scents of the African city were what filled his senses for the first seven years of his life.

For three months each summer, to escape the intense African heat, Christopher returned to England with his mother and younger brother. This journey was, in the nineteen thirties, before international travel became the commonplace activity it is today, a lengthy and exciting undertaking. First there was the train ride from Khartoum to Port Sudan, where the great liner would be waiting to carry them across the Red Sea and the Mediterranean. 'I still have vivid memories of being on those ships, of waking up and looking through the porthole to see that we'd arrived at Malta or somewhere, with all the sounds and smells of the port.'

His father's duties in the Sudan Political Service prevented him from accompanying his family on these annual summer leaves, so his children grew used to long periods without him. But fortunately his mother, unlike most colonial wives, was close to her children and usually present in their lives. 'She was the fixed point in a life which otherwise had a lot of movement. The security which comes from your mother being there, with consistent affection, was very important.'

His father, too, was to have a life-long influence on Christopher. He'd been one of that rare breed: the early, pre-First World War flyers, and a test pilot for Vickers, both before and during that war. 'It was horrendously dangerous; the wings used to fall off and that sort of thing – it was one crash after another. (That was how he'd met my mother – she was a nurse in the hospital where he was recovering after one of his crashes.) I don't think I'd be doing this job now [Chairman of the Civil Aviation Authority] but for the fact that I've always been fascinated by aviation because my father talked about it so much. I remember when I was about four or five there was a book called *Let's Go Flying* which I'd have read to me every single night. I never wanted any other book.'

Those early years in the Sudan helped to shape his later outlook on life. 'I think of myself as somebody who fits in reasonably comfortably in all kinds of environments, and I suppose that if you're exposed to very different scenes when you are very young, you don't necessarily accept just one thing as being the immutable norm. It makes you more adaptable and a bit less conventional than you might otherwise be. After all, if as a young child you're brought up with the sights and sounds and smells of Khartoum, you don't think that the world has always got to be like Woking.'

In the Sudan the Chataway family lived the traditional colonial life – a way of life belonging to the long-vanished era of the British Empire. They had several native servants, and Christopher was taught at home by English governesses. But in 1938, when he was seven, this changed dramatically – he moved back to England with his mother and brother, so that he could be enrolled at a boarding prep school. 'Although I always had a very good relationship with my mother, from the moment you go off to boarding school an inevitable distance comes between you which you never completely close again. From the age of eight I suddenly had to make my own way without her.'

He didn't really mind boarding – in that brutal *Lord of the Flies*-type environment, he was always 'somewhere at the top of the heap'. But he considers it all 'unnatural and uncivilized' – at least it was in those distant days, when pupils spent a great deal of time together unsupervised – and none of his own five children has ever attended boarding prep school.

He had to learn quickly how to survive at Forres Prep School, because mistakes were not easily forgotten or forgiven by the other boys. 'We had chamber-pots by our beds, and when I first arrived I thought that we were meant to use them. (Actually they were only there for emergencies.) Sometime during the first week I said to our Assistant Matron, "I've been in my potty, Miss Brown." Well, that was an appalling thing to say – no one there ever referred to them as "potties". And for several days afterwards the boys would call out to me in tones of derision, *"I've been in my potty, Miss Brown!"* '

When war broke out in 1939, Christopher's father was stranded in the Sudan. Lethal German U-boats made sailing home to England too risky. For three years they didn't see each other. Then, in the middle of the war, he returned permanently to work as a civil servant in London.

Christopher was eight at the outset of the war, and fourteen when it ended. So its dramas and tensions pervaded much of his childhood. The Headmaster of Forres was a clergyman who tended to relate the war's events to the Almighty. 'I can remember the headmaster addressing us at the time of the D-Day landings, when the weather was very bad, and saying, "At Dunkirk we were saved through God's help, because the weather was fine. The fact that the weather is now bad shows that God is not pleased with us." And we all felt *really* guilty; I remember thinking – what have I *done*, that He's gone and made the weather bad?'

Swanage was in a heavily bombed area. But Christopher was never frightened when, in the middle of the night, the air-raid sirens signalled another bombing raid. On the contrary – it was all very exciting. The boys would troop down into the cellars, delighted because they'd always be let off the first lesson in the morning as a result. The school was eventually evacuated to less hazardous Buckinghamshire. A year later the school chapel received a direct hit at a time of day when all the boys would have been in it. 'Perhaps the headmaster did have a direct line of communication with God!'

Christopher followed avidly the doings of the great wartime leader, Winston Churchill. 'I would hardly have acknowledged it at the time, but looking back now, the picture I had of myself when I went into politics was of me ending up as prime minister in a re-run of nineteen forty.'

But long before politics, there was running. Christopher had always been competent at games, but had never excelled at anything in particular. He'd been an indifferent sprinter, and it was by chance that he discovered at sixteen, as a pupil at Sherborne, that he was exceptionally gifted at long-distance running. He not only easily won his first half-mile race, but broke the junior record.

The school took little interest in athletics, so he acquired some books and taught himself how to train. At seventeen he entered the mile race in the national public schools' games, and came third. The following year he came second. After Sherborne came eighteen months of military service, during which time he won first the Army mile championship, and then the inter-services (Army/Navy/Air Force) championship. At nineteen he went to Oxford University, and by his second year there he'd made the British team, opening up the prospect of the Olympic Games.

For the next five years he immersed himself in his running career, becoming in the process a nationally celebrated figure, a fact which opened many doors to other worlds. 'When you're very well known for something, people make all kinds of other offers to you.' Commercial television had just started up in 1955; he and Robin Day became its first two newscasters.

He'd learnt a crucial lesson early in life, through his schooling: that there is a relationship between the amount of effort that you make and what you achieve. 'In running, this relationship is very direct: the more you train and the harder you try, the better you become. So it reinforced my belief that I had within me the capacity to improve myself. Perhaps not in everything – not singing or art, and not cricket, although *God* I tried hard at cricket, and I never made it past scorer for the third eleven!

'But it isn't necessary to be brilliant at everything. Each individual has some particular aptitude and what really matters is to discover it. This can only be done by trying as many different activities as possible. Although there is still a lot of deprivation, there are more opportunities for more children in Britain today than ever before. A child today has a great chance to find something which is going to be the doorway for the kind of life he wants to live.'

Peter Scudamore, MBE

'We had a nanny whom I hated, a horrible woman.
She disliked horses and didn't know anything
about them. So when my parents were away I'd
spend all my time on horseback – the one place
where she couldn't dominate me.'

Born in Hereford on 13 June 1958. Education: Hereford
Cathedral Prep School, Belmont Abbey School. Career:
Professional steeplechase jockey. Rider of over 1500 winners;
the only national hunt jockey to ride more than 200 winners
in one season (1988–89).

Peter grew up on his father's Herefordshire farm, surrounded by all types of horses and ponies. His father Michael was a famous steeplechaser in his prime – winner of the Grand National and the Cheltenham Gold Cup. After a serious fall ended his career in 1966, he turned to racehorse training.

'I had a very happy childhood. I've been riding virtually all my life, since I was put on a pony at about the age of three. I began to ride more seriously when I was eight; before that time my father had been a jockey, racing all over the place and I rarely saw him. But after his fall he was at home and we'd ride together. He didn't give me lessons, as such, it was just a part of life. We discussed horses at the dinner table, at the breakfast table . . .

'I had my own ponies and belonged to a pony club, taking part in endless competitions and events, races, show-jumping. Every weekend all through the summer we went to local gymkhanas. I remember many embarrassing moments when I went around a course the wrong way, missed a jump or made some other mistake. Once another rider and I galloped smack into each other during the "musical hats" event, and we both flew off our ponies.

'There were also some frightening moments – such as when I saw my father fall badly during training, and another time when my own pony fell down with me and cut its knee open. But nothing could put me off riding.

'For a while we had a nanny whom I hated, a horrible woman. She disliked horses and didn't know anything about them. So when my parents were away I'd spend all my time on horseback – the one place where she couldn't dominate me.

'By the time I was twelve I was riding the racehorses that my father trained at our stables. I don't think I was naturally gifted at riding, but I was persistent. And I always intended to be a jockey – it was a dream which turned into an ambition.

'My mother, always eager to "improve" me and my sister,

did all she could to dissuade me – she wanted me to get a *proper* job. National hunt racing is a very dangerous sport and she was always fearful for my safety. She used to fret over me constantly. As for my father, he used to tell me that if he had his time to do all over again, he'd do exactly the same.'

At the age of ten Peter was sent to a Catholic boarding school, where he was taught by Benedictine monks. 'I was smack down the middle academically, ending up with ten O levels and two A levels. But I never wanted to go on to university. It was sport that I enjoyed most of all, especially rugby.

'It was a relief when I reached the sixth form and was allowed to grow my hair long and put my hands in my pockets. I was groomed to be head boy, but obviously wasn't quite capable of it. Instead, I was deputy head boy for two years running. It was the cushiest job in the school – I had no responsibilities, just power and privilege. The headmaster was a sportsman and I always got on extremely well with him. But I didn't like being at an all-boys school; it made me very insecure where girls were concerned. It was a false environment for a youngster to be growing up in.

'Because I always wanted to ride for a living, I considered school almost a waste of time. Now, looking back on it, I can see it's done me a lot of good. It gave me the ability to concentrate and taught me to work hard. Although I wasn't really set up for school life, the monks were good to me and I respected their way of life.'

Between the ages of ten and eighteen, while Peter was at boarding school, most of his riding was done during the school holidays. He was competent on horseback, sometimes a mite over-confident, and liked to be flashy at competitions. He'd imitate flat race jockeys – particularly his great idol, Lester Piggott – with their very short stirrups, because it looked good. But this superficial approach began to change in his teens as he realized that it was Piggott's quiet professionalism, not the length of his stirrups, which were worthy of emulation.

'My father taught me so much about riding – how to behave, never to miss a trick, and that I owed it to myself to do my best, to make the most of every opportunity that came my way. He never bossed me about; he moulded me in the most gentle way. He never raised his voice.

'On the other hand, we never discussed school at home. School and home were totally separate, a million miles apart. I remember after one holiday turning up back at school to do A levels without any idea which A levels I was going to do – not a clue.'

When he left school, to placate his mother, he got a 'proper' job in an estate agent's office. It was a line of business that her own family had been involved in, and it was her idea. So he left home and for a year made the tea, licked stamps, put up signposts and ran errands – and was bored to death, except when he rode in races in his spare time. His boss told him he wasn't hard enough to be a jockey. 'There were a lot of people in the office I didn't like, and I'd think to myself – today you've got me making the tea, but one day you'll all be pleased to have known me!'

That day came soon enough. At nineteen he went into racing full-time – initially as an amateur, turning professional a year later. He was successful virtually from the beginning, with his first national hunt win at the age of twenty. 'I owe that in part to the legacy from my father, an honest, well-respected jockey, who gave me a good name which got me going very quickly.'

It was now, as his career in this dangerous sport took off, that his monastic schooling and the religious aspect of his life gave him a much-needed inner strength. 'A prayer before a particularly challenging race can settle my mind, put me at ease with myself and give me the courage to face it. Naturally I'm afraid of getting hurt, like anyone else would be.' He may be a practising Catholic, but he doesn't pray for divine protection against the dire physical risks of steeplechasing. In any case, that would be useless; he's taken many spills and broken a lot of bones already.

'A jockey friend of mine once went into a church before a big, important race. He lit a candle and prayed, "God, please help me win this race – not for my sake, not for the money, but for the *horse*." I guess he thought that angle would appeal more to the Almighty.'

He looks back affectionately at an idyllic youth spent on horseback in the English countryside he loves. As a young-ster his closest companions included the ponies and horses he grew up with on the family farm. 'I had two special ponies, Black Opal and Bobby. And I recall racehorses that were so majestic, so powerful, yet so gentle. We had an unforgettable one called O'Creave. He learnt how to slide open the bolts to his stall and he'd come out and have an amble around the yard. He was a real character with a sense of humour.'

His record-breaking success has put him into the media limelight and brought him into contact with the sporting elite, not least of all that passionate rider, the Princess Royal. But his mother hasn't stopped worrying and fussing over him. 'She still wants to know when I'm going to get a proper job.'

Judy Blume

'I was a good girl . . . It's a hard way to grow up, feeling you've always got to please everybody and be good.'

Born Judy Sussman in Elizabeth, New Jersey, USA on 2 December 1938. Education: Victor Mravlag Elementary School, Hamilton Junior High School, Battin High School (all in Elizabeth, NJ), New York University. Career: Writer of 22 books, including: *Are You There God? It's Me, Margaret*, *It's Not the End of the World*, *Deenie*, *Forever*, *Tales of a Fourth Grade Nothing*, *Tiger Eyes*, *Then Again, Maybe I Won't*.

y father was a dentist, the youngest of seven. While I was growing up all of his brothers and sisters died – this was a very important part of my childhood. We just seemed to go from one funeral to another, and in the Jewish religion each wake would last a week. There would be draped mirrors and mourners sitting around on little orange crates, fruit baskets would arrive and people would come and pinch my cheek and say, "How are you? I haven't seen you since the last funeral."

'We weren't a religious family, on the whole. We went to synagogue a couple of times a year, on the high holy days. But to us it was just a bit of fun, it meant getting dressed up, wearing hats and new shoes. For me religion has nothing to do with being in a church or synagogue, it's a private relationship with God or some other being.

'Religion is what sets you apart from other people, and I wasn't really touched by it until someone called me a name. As a senior in high school, I once went out on a date with a young Texan who'd never met a Jew. When he found out I was Jewish he went off me immediately. He wouldn't kiss me or even touch me anymore. I found that very shocking.

'Last autumn I was speaking at a convention, which was followed by a book-signing. A man came over and asked me to sign a book and his name sounded familiar. I asked, "Do you know me?" And he said, "Of course I do; that's why I'm here." He was that old date of mine from Texas, now a balding man of fifty-something. We fell into each other's arms and cried. It was an incredible reunion.

'My mother was a housewife, very practical. She was shy and anxious and quiet, we never really talked about anything. But my father and I were very close. He was the opposite of my mother, so alive and exciting. His philosophy was "go for it!". He loved life and knew how to have a good time. He'd sing to all his patients as they sat in the chair, he'd tell them jokes. Everyone adored my father. People sometimes made appointments just to come and talk to him at his office.

'My father was the one I wanted to be with. Instead of being in the kitchen with my mother, I'd be down in the basement workshop helping my father, with hammer and nails. My older brother and I had a sort of non-relationship. We've always been totally different from each other. I was the one who always wanted to please, he was the difficult one, the "problem child" – my parents didn't know what to do with him. I think he hated me.

'I was a good girl. I did well in school, I never made trouble. It's a hard way to grow up, feeling you've always got to please everybody and be good. Eventually something's got to give. And my own adolescent rebellion (which I should have had at sixteen) eventually rose to the surface when I was thirty-five! By then of course I was married and had children. It's a terrible thing to go through an adolescent rebellion at that age and drag your children through it with you, but I did. I came out of it at about forty.

'I suffered from severe eczema from the age of six months. When I was thirteen I had a particularly bad time, because I was allergic to an ointment which they gave me. My face swelled and my eyes closed up – I was a mess. I had elephant skin up and down my whole body. I outgrew it in the end, more or less, but I still have occasional itchiness in the winter.

'Besides that problem, I was plagued by the usual adolescent angst. But my role in life was to "be happy", so I kept most of it buried, I would never share it with anyone, which was a big mistake. That's why I went crazy later on, in a desperate attempt to find myself at last.

'I had two enormously important years, when I was nine and ten. Because of an illness my brother had at the time, my mother took us to live in Miami Beach, Florida. I tasted a freedom there I'd never known before. My father naturally had to stay behind and carry on working, and I missed him terribly, but for some reason my mother changed during that time. She was less anxious; maybe she was better away from my father, I don't know.

'I loved my life in Florida, it was so much looser. I was outdoors all the time, I could come and go as I pleased. I was the new kid at school, but there were a lot of "winter kids" there, like us, from October to June. It's funny to talk about romance for a nine- or ten-year-old, but it *was* a romantic period of my life – it was warm and sultry, there was a lot of good fun, I loved various boys in my class. Something fundamental happened to me there; when I came back I was no longer shy.

'I became ritualistic while we lived there: there were certain prayers I always said for my father, and I made up a list of things I'd have to do daily in order to preserve his health and safety. (I took that on as my own personal burden, as I was always aware of how his brothers and sisters were dying young, one by one – most children don't experience death so often.) By the time I got to high school this had all changed, and if my books tend to be about the years of childhood rather than high school, it's because I'm fascinated much more by the *child* I was, than the teenager. I identify most strongly with the period just before adolescence. It seemed to me at that point in life that everything was possible. In high school, things no longer seemed quite as possible. And by early adulthood, they were *im*possible. But this is an individual thing – everyone identifies with a different period of his or her life.

'I went to summer camp in Connecticut every year from the age of eleven to fourteen, and that, like Florida, was also a very freeing experience. There was nobody to say "don't do it". You had to fend for yourself, to make it work. You could taste things and try things and find out more about who you were. You didn't have to report to someone every day.

'Throughout my childhood I invented stories. I'd never write them down. They were intended for no one else, just me. I spent hours and hours outside bouncing a ball against the wall, thinking up the most wonderful, melodramatic tales. I played with dolls, too, for a very long time. But I wasn't interested in the dolls themselves, they were really the "puppets" for my stories.

'Writing came easily to me, whenever I had to do it in school, but we weren't encouraged to do much creative writing. I did write for the school magazine, but I also enjoyed being in school plays, singing, dancing. When I grew up, married and had kids, and all those creative outlets no longer existed for me, I was desperate to find something through which I could express myself – it was a need I knew I had to satisfy in some way. I began writing seriously at the age of twenty-seven, out of this desperation.

'I took a part-time evening course in creative writing. My teacher wasn't much of a writer herself, but she gave me the most important gift she could give – support and encouragement. I had two years of constant rejections for the stories (mostly rhyming children's stories) that I was writing. But then I began to get published.

'I was still living in suburban New Jersey, where I'd lived all my life, married to a man who was also from New Jersey. It was the life my mother had always wanted me to live, just like her own. But it was not far from New York City, with all its excitements and possibilities, so I was able to taste another kind of life, too.

'When I think about that suburban life now, I get stomach pains. I could never go back to a suburb. I didn't know anything else while I was growing up, so I thought it was great. The only alternative I experienced was when I'd sometimes spend the weekend with friends I'd met at summer camp, who lived in Manhattan. I was really impressed that you could have anything you wanted delivered. If you needed a toothbrush, you'd send out for one and someone would actually deliver it to your door. And I loved walking along Broadway, seeing the crowds, the lights. It was all great fun, but it never occurred to me then that I'd live anywhere but in suburban New Jersey.'

Judy found the role of suburban housewife about as comfortable as a straitjacket. The other housewives of the neighbourhood, not one of whom worked, viewed her writing with suspicion. It was an abnormality they couldn't comprehend – what was wrong with her, why wasn't she content? As she began to achieve success, this resentment increased. Did she think she was better than the rest of them?

Eventually she left that world behind to seek another, with the immense courage needed to step out into the unknown. Perhaps her father's philosophical legacy had something to do with it: 'Go for it – do it.' For Judy, liberation has brought great personal and professional success. Talent and determination are a winning combination, but they must first be given the freedom to thrive.

Rt Revd Roy Williamson, Bishop of Southwark

'I officiated at two weddings there, and both times I wore my football gear underneath my cassock and ran from the church straight down to the sports field.'

Born in Belfast, Northern Ireland on 18 December 1932. Education: Ravenscroft Public Elementary School, Elmgrove Public Elementary School, Oak Hill Theological College. Career: Ordained as an Anglican priest in 1963; made Bishop of Bradford, 1984; Bishop of Southwark since 1992.

I grew up in Bloomfield, a Protestant, inner city district of Belfast. My father was Protestant, but my mother was Roman Catholic. Mixed marriages were very rare in those days, and it says a lot for my mother's character that she became a kind of matriarch for the entire neighbourhood, a trusted confidante. Whenever anyone was ill, or needed help of any kind, she was sent for – sometimes in the middle of the night. She held the keys to practically every house in the neighbourhood.

'My childhood was extremely happy. We were fairly poor, but there were always people coming and going at our house, there was a lot of laughter, life had a wonderful rhythm. I was never lonely: as the youngest of fourteen kids you couldn't be lonely if you tried. We lived in a three-bedroomed terraced house with an outdoor loo, no electricity, no garden. By the time I came along, some of my older siblings had moved out, but even so we had to sleep two, sometimes three to a bed. My clothes and shoes were hand-me-downs, but I never thought the worse of them for that.

'My father had been a shipyard worker at Harland and Wolff, but a serious injury when he was young left him a semi-invalid, so I only ever remember him working as a garage attendant – it was the only job he could do. But there was no trace of bitterness in him. He was a lovely, delightful man.

'My mother was my closest companion. She was incredible – so full of life and fun. She'd been disowned by her wealthy family for marrying both out of her religion and out of her class. And for my father, the fact that his wife was Catholic made him open to suspicion and ridicule. I recollect the anxiety in our family if my father was late coming home from work. There were no terrorist outrages when I was a youngster, but there was a lot of sectarian tension.

'As a lad I became aware – it was part of folklore – that there were certain roads I mustn't ever walk down, predominantly Catholic roads. When my Protestant school played football against a Catholic school, it was very much a needle game, we fully expected to have stones thrown at us afterwards, and vice versa. Even as an adult, when you went to a football match with a Protestant team playing a Catholic team, you had to be careful to leave amongst the right crowd.

'As kids we had our ritualistic gang battles – we threw stones at each other – but only because it was expected of us, it was part of growing up, it didn't involve any hatred. I suppose we were brainwashed, in a way. We didn't appreciate that the Roman Catholics didn't have our advantages. I can see that now, with the perspective of distance. For a very long time I wasn't even aware that my own mother was Catholic. My parents didn't raise the question of religion at home. There was a lot of love between them, and that was all that mattered.'

The first key turning point in Roy's life came when he was eleven. Not too interested in the academic side of school, his great love was football. He was small and thin, but an agile player. His skill at the sport came to the fore during a three-week nature study school trip, during which several football games were organized.

'There were about a hundred pupils on the trip. I remember very well the headmaster telling us that there were some talented footballers amongst us and that it was time we formed a school football team. He read out the names of the eleven players he wanted in the team, and Williamson was one of them. That was, for me, the first public recognition that I had something to offer. An important moment.

'Football became central to my life. Our team won not only the local schools cup, but the Ulster and the Irish schools cups. I played alongside Billy Bingham, who eventually went on to play for Ireland and is currently the Irish team manager. At thirteen, during my final year at school, I captained the school team (although I was the smallest one in it).

'For a while I wanted to be a professional player, but

although I never took it up, I continued playing for many years to a reasonably high level as an amateur. I built up something of a reputation, I suppose, because when I was ordained and sent to be curate of All Saints Church in Crowborough, East Sussex, I was immediately invited to join the town team. I later became its captain. This was a bit tricky, because one of my parish duties was to take weddings which, like football matches, were held on Saturday afternoons. I officiated at two weddings there, and both times I wore my football gear underneath my cassock and ran from the church straight down to the sports field.

'I've never been able to understand why people divide things sharply into the spiritual and the secular. I was brought up to believe that life is an interwoven whole, and for me, playing football is as spiritual as going to church.'

Roy left school at fourteen, as did all his siblings. His first job was as messenger boy for a drapery shop. Then, instead of following his brothers into the shipyards, he took on an apprenticeship at a local boot and shoe manufacturer, eventually becoming an itinerant salesman for the company.

His parish church – St Donard's, Bloomfield – provided more than mere spiritual guidance. It was the hub of the family's social and leisure life, too, with its youth clubs, scout movement and organized sports activities. Roy sang in the choir. 'On Sunday evenings, after the service, it was the tradition for everyone to walk up into the hills around the city. Everything was closed, there was nowhere else to go, so us teenagers, boys and girls together, walked and talked, had fun – the roads were dense with young people.'

At nineteen Roy had an experience (the second big turning point) which converted him from a passive to an active Christian. He attended a series of talks given by Revd Keith de Berry which resulted in intensive soul-searching. 'I realized that until then my faith had been superficial; now I felt a call to engage my mind and emotions more directly. It was a revelation.'

107

A few years later, as a door-to-door evangelist with the London City Mission, he found that his years as shoe salesman had been the best possible training. 'It taught me how to deal with people. I had been a shy youngster, but I learnt as a sales rep how to walk into a roomful of strangers, start a conversation and get through to them. Selling Christianity – when you knock on a door and have about ten seconds to make an impact – is really no different. I love people, and have no difficulty with them.'

He got his O levels in his late-twenties through a correspondence course, then studied for the priesthood at Oak Hill College. His lack of formal education did not stop him from rising through the ranks of the Church. But even so, he thought 'the Lord was playing a joke' on him when in 1984 out of the blue the Prime Minister, Margaret Thatcher, invited him to be Bishop of Bradford – the only Anglican bishop at the time who had never been to university.

'My mixed Protestant–Catholic parentage was of immense value to me in Bradford, a city with a huge Muslim population. Great tensions divided the community during the Salman Rushdie affair and the Gulf War. But I had long ago recognized that there are always two sides to an argument. Because I reject the "them and us" mentality and wage a one-man war against stereotyping, I was able to do some positive things in breaking down the barriers.'

Naim Attallah

'I smoked like mad, regularly gambled away half my monthly allowance and played all kinds of tricks, making my uncle's life a misery.'

Born in Haifa, Palestine, on 1 May 1931. Education: Dames de Nazareth convent primary school and College des Frères (both in Haifa), Battersea Polytechnic. Career: Book publisher, magazine proprietor, film and theatrical producer, parfumier, chief executive of Asprey plc, managing director of Mappin & Webb, managing director of Watches of Switzerland.

aim Attallah came to this country as a penniless teenager. Today he is a successful and high-profile business entrepreneur, at home amongst the famous – and one of the best-known Arabs in London.

He was born into the Palestine of the British Mandate. It was a land which had finally emerged after the First World War from four centuries of domination by the Ottoman Turks and, understandably, did not take kindly to British control. Civil war raged as the Palestinians struggled for independence. They were dangerous, unstable times.

Naim grew up at the centre of a big, predominantly female household including his mother, three sisters, two grandmothers and a great-aunt. A cherished 'only son', he was cosseted and fussed over to an astounding degree. He'd been sickly as a small child, and ever after the family treated him as a frail and delicate creature – checking him all through the night to make sure he was covered, bathing him, doing everything for him. ('Even when I was practically grown up women bathed me, like in Paradise.') Sometimes the women servants of the house spent the whole night cuddling the little boy, so he shouldn't feel lonely. Small wonder that the adult Naim is most comfortable in the company of women.

Being constantly pampered did not, however, make for a happy childhood. 'I wasn't a happy child, because I was virtually a prisoner. I wasn't allowed to go out and play with other boys. I was never taught to swim. I still can't, to this day. I wasn't allowed to ride a bicycle. These were all considered dangerous activities from which I had to be protected.' On one occasion, after much haggling, he was reluctantly permitted to go on a picnic with some other kids. He was accidentally hit on the head with a rock and needed several stitches, which put paid to any future outings for Naim.

'One of my most vivid childhood memories is of sitting for hours on the balcony of our third-floor flat in Haifa, overlooking a busy main road, and watching the world go by, yearning for some space, some freedom. But I was never allowed out, the family was always worried that I would get run over, or do myself an injury. This sense of being kept almost in solitary confinement was what upset me most as a child. Adventure was not on the menu for me. I think I've compensated for this in adult life by becoming extremely adventurous in business.'

Not surprisingly, his greatest heroes were the swashbuckling film stars of the thirties and forties, especially Errol Flynn – virile and audacious men who spent all their time engaged in swordfights, saving damsels, jousting, scaling castle walls, and generally outwitting the bad guys.

'Not very often, but once in a while I was taken to a very decent cinema in the Jewish quarter of Haifa. My favourite film was Alexander Korda's *The Thief of Baghdad*, with Sabu. I queued for hours to see it.'

His father was Chief Cashier for Barclays Bank in Haifa, responsible for paying the salaries of the British Armed Forces during the Second World War. He was strong-willed, often aggressive, and the rest of the family was afraid of his temper. He and Naim were never close. 'I didn't inherit much of his character. He was a pessimist, and I have always been optimistic.'

The Attallahs were a religious Roman Catholic family, and Naim attended first a convent school, where the nuns were kind and loving, and like the women in his family pampered their 'little Naim', and then a high school run by monks of the order of St Jean Baptiste de Lasalle: 'We led a spartan existence at that school – the monks were very tough, very strict. We had to go to mass every day, and to confession.' He didn't have pleasant memories of the monks, 'but the nuns were marvellous'. At both schools he was taught in French, so he was brought up bilingual in French and Arabic; English came later.

'I'm not religious now, in the formal sense, but my

upbringing has given me a sense of spirituality. I still get a feeling of serenity whenever I enter a church.'

Perhaps because he was so over-protected and restricted physically, he had a vibrant inner life. At the age of nine, with the Second World War in full swing, he spent an entire summer vacation producing his own daily newspaper concerned with the progress of the war. He kept abreast of the latest events by listening avidly to every radio station he could receive – to the BBC Overseas Service, to the broadcasts from occupied France, to Hitler's speeches: 'which had me totally mesmerized'. He sold his Arabic-language paper, complete with regular commentaries, to all his parents' friends, who thought him terribly clever and predicted that he would go far.

Was it his ambition even then to be a publisher? 'I wanted to be a journalist – I didn't know then what a publisher was. I had a nose for news from an early age. I always loved the written word, and I was very articulate. That was the most rewarding aspect of my youth.'

He didn't, in the end, pursue this childhood goal, but has remained fascinated by the world of newspapers and journalists, with which he is closely associated today.

When Naim was sixteen his parents decided to take him out of school and send him away from Haifa, where daily life was becoming increasingly perilous. ('My entire childhood was spent surrounded by violence and war – first it was the Arabs against the British, then the Jews against the British, then the Jews and the Arabs against each other. No wonder I'm a pacifist.') Together with his paternal grandmother he went to live in more peaceful Nazareth. There his life changed radically. At last the 'imprisoned' boy got his first taste of freedom.

Not only was he spared having to attend school ('I just read books on my own'), but he developed an undying attachment to his grandmother, who he regards as the most influential and inspiring figure of his youth. 'She was illiterate, but so very wise – close to nature, a real "woman of the earth". We went to bed at dusk and rose with the Morning Star. I helped with the chores, and she told me tales of the First World War, when the Allies and the Arabs joined forces to rout the Turks. As young women, she and her sister had watched the Turkish soldiers retreating across the hills, then raided their stores of provisions, carrying home great sacks of flour.'

From someone who'd barely been allowed outside, Naim turned into a kind of Arab Huckleberry Finn, a freewheeling country youth, doing target practice with a rifle he'd found (shooting holes in his grandmother's great earthenware water jug).

'I was twenty-three when she died, but I still think of her often.'

In 1948 the British Mandate for Palestine ended, the new State of Israel was born. The following year, aged eighteen and determined that the days of watching the world go by from the balcony were over, Naim announced his intention to go abroad to study. His parents, ever fearful for him, were discouraging. But he could no longer be contained. He had an uncle living in London, and it was arranged that Naim could stay with him.

He was apprehensive when he arrived. After all, his previous experience of the British did not exactly inspire confidence or affection: he recalls several occasions in his early childhood when British soldiers, rounding up locals in response to the latest act of insurgency, barged into his home and removed his entire family at bayonet point to some place of detention. He grew up thinking that the British were brutal and uncivilized.

'I was pleasantly surprised to find that no one in London pushed you around with bayonets. In fact, all my impressions were positive. I even found the notorious London "pea soup" fog a fascinating new adventure; it was thrilling to get lost and spend three hours trying to find your way back home. And I fell in love with English girls, finding them less sophisticated, but more relaxing than the foreign ones. It was a *bonanza*.'

He went a bit overboard with his new-found freedom. His uncle was a scant ten years older than him, a mature student of engineering at the Battersea Polytechnic (where Naim was also rapidly enrolled), and he had no control over the wild teenager. 'The first thing I did was to acquire that forbidden item: a bicycle. I smoked like mad, regularly gambled away half my monthly allowance and played all kinds of tricks, making my uncle's life a misery. Once, in a burst of good-natured fun, I blew up the chimney with fireworks and nearly burnt the place down.

'Whenever there was any kind of commotion at the Poly and my uncle asked who was the cause of it, he was always told, "Your nephew!" It was quite funny, really.'

Eventually, Naim's money stopped coming, he was unable to finish his course, and he had to take on whatever unskilled jobs he could find. Thus began five years of hard physical toil, which, for someone who'd never even had to bath himself back home, came as a terrible shock.

At last he took on a clerical job in a bank. He didn't really want it, but it was better than getting agonizing blisters on his hands from tying ropes on riverboats. When one of the bank's foreign exchange dealers fell ill and Naim was suddenly given the chance to take over, his career was launched. He'd been watching and absorbing all that went on around him, so no one had to teach him anything – it was as though he'd been doing the job for years.

In 1972 he decided to go it alone. He started from scratch, borrowing money to set himself up as a freelance entrepreneur, putting together financial deals for which he had an obvious talent. He became a publisher in 1976, when he bought Quartet Books. Today he is one of London's few remaining independent publishers, and undoubtedly the quirkiest – a refreshing antidote to the vast international conglomerates which now dominate publishing.

'I don't believe that in order to be successful you have to be in the right place at the right time. We are all in the right place at the right time – it's just that some of us perceive it and others don't. I also know that, although the world is a jungle where the fittest survive, you don't have to be ruthless, to tread all over people, in order to get to the top. You only need to have a vision, to be determined and to work hard.

'Each individual is master of his own destiny. And the rate of success is higher among the poor, the have-nots. Why? Because if you're hungry – I don't mean only physically, but hungry for knowledge, for success, for everything – you make a real effort, you go out and satisfy your hunger. Don't tell me that the one who is born rich is also more intelligent – *that* God didn't do.'

·*Dame Barbara Cartland*

'All the men wanted to take me out. Often they would say, "I will shoot myself if you do not marry me!" That was quite normal in those days.'

Born in Peopleton, Worcestershire, on 9 July 1901. Education: Private governesses, Worcester High School for Girls, Malvern College for Girls, Netley Abbey Finishing School. Career: Record-breaking romantic novelist. Author of 557 books; over 600 million copies sold in countries all over the world.

Barbara Cartland's childhood at the beginning of this century would seem most unreal to those growing up now, at the end of it. Those years in rural England before and even during the First World War were tranquil, innocent and romantic for a young girl enjoying the privileges of aristocratic society.

That's not to say that everything was always easy: in 1903, when Barbara was two, her wealthy financier grandfather James Cartland lost a lot of money in a national financial crisis and shot himself. Her father Bertram lost the fortune he was due to inherit and had to settle for a much more modest lifestyle for his family.

But all was not lost. 'Our lives were always busy. We had a piano and Mother used to play to us, we sang songs, we were read to all the time – fairy tales and religious books. I remember our first gramophone, which was very exciting; the only song I can remember hearing on it was *Little Willy's Wild Woodbines* (rather an odd one to remember).

'We had an enormous garden in Pershore filled with beautiful blossoming plum trees; I was quite certain that there were fairies amongst them. And I used to listen at the trunks of big trees to hear the goblins underneath them. I really believed in all that, which was far better than believing the ghastly things children now see on the television, which are very bad for them.

'But reading is the most important thing – I have always loved to read – and it is what stops a person going gaga in old age. I have many friends who are all senile because they never read a book.'

There was no television, cinema or radio, but there were plenty of children's parties in the great old country houses – Elmley Castle, Croome Court, Madresfield Court – where Barbara played musical chairs and hunt the slipper with the grandchildren of earls and countesses, and where the 'house ghost' was almost compulsory.

'I was always going to stay in big houses; all our friends

117

had big houses in those days. During the war when my father was fighting in Flanders I was sent to live in Nailsea Court, a large haunted house in Somerset, to share a governess with a girl of my own age. We were thirteen. There were all sorts of ghosts there, it was rather frightening, but we had a lovely time. Naturally we learnt very little, but then girls were not required to have an education, they were brought up to get married and behave like a Lady.

'At finishing school I remember the headmistress would sometimes read us little bits out of *The Times*, but we were never allowed to read the paper ourselves. Do not ask me why. The school had no library, either. I learnt nothing.'

What was she like as a youngster? 'Intelligent, vivacious, pretty. I was very upset because my hair was dead straight and it was the fashion then to have curly hair. I used to have it done up in rags every night, and always before I went to a party. Of course in those days you went to parties in a brougham [horse-drawn carriage], rather slowly. As we drove up the drive my mother would take the rags out and comb my hair, but by the time we arrived it was straight again. My hair only became naturally curly after I had started to take vitamins as an adult.

'One always had a chaperone in those days – usually your mother or your governess – one wasn't allowed to rush about on one's own. Girls and boys never mixed unless they were fully chaperoned. Once, when I was sixteen, I somehow found myself alone with a midshipman who said he wanted to kiss me. I said "Certainly not".'

In 1919, just after the war, eighteen-year-old Barbara left school and 'came out'. Her father, after four years in the trenches, had been killed in action the year before. The family lost its home and Barbara's mother took her and her two younger brothers to live in London, where they rented a furnished house in South Kensington. Barbara adored the 'wildly exciting' capital.

In line with the conventions of the day, the young debutante was now permitted to have male escorts . . . up to a point. 'You were not allowed to dine alone with a man. That was considered *fast*. On the other hand, you could dance with him until six in the morning. What the difference was I cannot think, but it suited the men very well, because they did not have much money. They were mostly young Guardsmen, so they would dine at the Guards' club, which was cheap, then afterwards pick me up in their white tie and tails and we would dance all night – the foxtrot, the two-step, the waltz. It was all frightfully good exercise.

'And there was lovely music – we heard Geraldo's Band, Ambrose's Band. You could dance all night at the Berkeley, a *very* smart place, for only ten shillings. The man would drink a beer and the woman would have a sort of "cup", rather nasty, with strawberries floating in it. I never drank alcohol until I was twenty-three.'

She had her first proposal of marriage nine days after she left school, from a forty-year-old moustachioed colonel. 'He seemed so old I thought he was practically falling into his grave; naturally I refused.' (She had forty-nine proposals in all, until she finally accepted the fiftieth when she was twenty-five.)

'I was a huge success. All the men wanted to take me out. Often they would say, "I will shoot myself if you do not marry me!" That was quite normal in those days. Angus Bowes-Lyon shot himself for my best friend; that was *very* uncomfortable. You see, men had just been through the war and thought nothing of death. Life was short and unimportant.

'One night I was flirting with one of my young men in a taxi, and he suddenly produced a revolver and said, "Unless you say you will marry me I shall shoot myself here and now!" I thought he was going to shoot *me* – I was terrified. We argued, then I said I would give him an answer when he had taken me home. When we got there I jumped out of the taxi and said "No!", rushed into the house and slammed the door. He did not shoot himself that night, but he did some years later.

'Men treated you like a piece of Dresden china. They asked your permission to kiss you; they never touched you in any other way. They never told you a dirty story or anything like that. You were precious, a Lady. They told you how lovely and marvellous you were.'

Barbara had become one of the Bright Young Things of the nineteen twenties, the era of the Flapper Girl and the dance called the Charleston. People wanted to forget the war and its tragedies, so they lost themselves in an abundance of gaiety.

It was during a family holiday one summer, when Barbara had left all her young men in London and was 'bored sick of the country', that she chanced upon her future career. Her brother, still a pupil at Charterhouse, told her to shut up one day because he had some essays to write. 'Oh, all right,' said Barbara, 'then *I* shall write a novel.' One of the Coventrys came to lunch (it was from the Earl of Coventry that the Cartlands rented their house in Pershore after the family fortune was lost) and Mrs Cartland remarked proudly, 'Barbara is writing a *novel*.' He wanted to hear it.

'I read out the first two chapters, and he said, "Very good, indeed. Finish it." But they all said to each other, "Ha, ha, ha – she never will." I thought I most certainly *will*. It annoyed me that they thought I could not do anything.'

Jigsaw was published in 1923, and described as 'Mayfair with the lid off'. It ran into six editions and was translated into five languages. It was innocent stuff by today's standards, but because the villain kissed the heroine, her great-aunts never spoke to her again. It was the first of an astoundingly long line of romantic novels which ultimately gained Barbara the title, 'Queen of Romance'.

A strong sense of Christian morality lies at the heart of all her five hundred and fifty-seven books. 'I was always very religious; my family was Anglo-Catholic – very High Church.

My mother was an ardent believer; she had been brought up much more strictly than we were and considered my generation rather fast.'

Barbara writes more books per year (an average of twenty-three) than any other author in the world. Where do the plots come from? 'As soon as I finish a book, I pray to God and say, "Please God, I want a plot". The next morning I wake up and have a plot. His ideas are so much better than mine. But you cannot talk about God to the English, they get too embarrassed.

'Women's Lib has taken away the Bible from everybody. It has taken the Beauty and the Romance out of life. Women now are all supposed to want careers, but what a woman really was born for was to make a man happy in marriage and have children. And all these mixed schools today are a great mistake. It is the girls who cause most of the trouble, chasing after the boys, and interrupting the most important thing, which is their education. It is terribly difficult for a boy to get on at school with all these girls fiddling around him.'

Barbara Cartland makes it perfectly clear that she prefers males to females, so it surprised me to receive a friendly kiss on the cheek in place of a business-like handshake, as we parted at the door of her country mansion. Perhaps, as with her little white Pekinese, Mai-Mai, the bark is worse than the bite.

Ken Livingstone, MP

'If somebody like me can get to Parliament,
anyone can.'

Born in Streatham, London, on 17 June 1945. Education: St
Leonard's Primary, Tulse Hill Comprehensive, Philippa
Fawcett College of Education. Career: Laboratory technician in
cancer research institute; joined Labour Party in 1969 and
entered local government politics in 1971; leader of Greater
London Council 1981–86; MP for Brent East since 1987.

y parents were a devoted, loving couple. My father had been a merchant sailor, then became a window cleaner, and my mother was a music hall dancer. It was a classic tale of love at first sight. In fact they were so happy just being together that they didn't feel any need to have children – I was an accident.' His mother thought he looked so unsightly when he was born that she covered his head with a blanket whenever she took him out in his pram.

His parents decided to have a second child so that little Ken shouldn't be spoilt – hence, a sister appeared. 'I managed to be spoilt, anyway, growing up in a home environment which was close-knit and secure. My parents were still just as much in love with each other when my father died in nineteen seventy-one, as on the day they got married.'

The Livingstones struggled to make ends meet, to pay the mortgage, to get by on a modest working-class income. But they managed to have a holiday each year, and the children never had to 'go without'.

Ken, however, didn't like being a child. He'd been born small and weak, then nearly died at the age of three during a gastro-enteritis epidemic; his recovery was a long, slow process. A bad eater, too, he was always the 'runt' of the class. 'I wasn't a terribly attractive prospect as far as girls were concerned.'

Added to these personal self-doubts and worries was something more basic: the lack of confidence which Ken claims is congenital amongst working-class youngsters. 'Middle-class kids have always been educated to lead; self-confidence is instilled in them from the beginning. But working-class kids are generally told what they can *not* do. They're educated merely to be disciplined, kept in order, and as a preparation for work. That's how our class system operates.

'When I speak to students at a school like Eton or Harrow, they talk about what they would do if they were Chancellor of the Exchequer, how they'd change the tax laws, etc. When

I was their age, I would have been too frightened to walk into a bank. But I do think the comprehensive system has given working-class kids a tremendous advantage that they didn't have before – it's boosted their confidence.'

Instinctively anti-authoritarian, Ken yearned to be an adult, to be independent, free of the confines of school life, which he loathed . . . until 1956, when, at the age of eleven, he came under the guidance of a young English teacher and form master called Philip Hobsbaum. It was a great stroke of luck. Hobsbaum was the single most influential figure throughout Ken's schooling, an exceptionally progressive teacher who challenged and inspired the weedy little boy.

'Teachers like him have always been very rare. He got the best out of me. I'd been an academic disaster, I'd failed my eleven-plus. But under Hobsbaum I ended up at the top of the class, a couple of terms running. He was my teacher for only one year, but I was never the same again afterwards: I'd been taught how to think for myself.'

Ken's first term under Hobsbaum marked a major turn-ing point for him, because it was this exceptional teacher who first made the future politician aware of politics. In the autumn of 1956 the Soviet army brutally crushed the Hungarian Uprising; it was an event which shocked the democratic world. In Mr Hobsbaum's English class at Tulse Hill Comprehensive, two boys were chosen to stand up and debate the issue. Speaking against the Soviet invasion was Ken Livingstone – it was the first world event in which he took an avid interest.

'Through him I became aware of politics, generally – I wasn't committed to any ideology, but it became an inter-esting subject to argue about.' Hobsbaum was himself a Bevanite – an adherent of Nye Bevan, the radical-left Labour leader who designed the National Health Service after World War Two. His political philosophy was not lost on the young Ken.

Hobsbaum's class also debated the other big event of that

autumn, the Suez Crisis, in which Britain and France launched a joint military offensive against Egypt (Ken, his 'gift of the gab' by now well-established, argued against that, too). Afterwards they staged a mock general election, with Ken as Liberal candidate. 'If the teaching profession was filled with people like that, the academic ability of the population would probably treble.'

Like most kids, Ken initially adopted his parents' broad political views; they were traditional working-class Tories. He was even in favour of hanging. He didn't really begin to form his own political ideas until he left school at seventeen. He was the first member of his family, on both sides, not to vote Conservative. For many years, though, he had a scathing contempt for all politicians.

'The personality traits which today make me an awkward and difficult politician, made me an awkward and difficult child at school: I was never prepared to accept anybody's authority unless I was convinced that it was just and correct. I questioned everything I was told and preferred to take the minority viewpoint, even if I was in a minority of one . . . that's why I was always in trouble.'

This was, in part, a legacy from Hobsbaum, who had taught his pupils to be confident in their own opinions and not to assume that they had to accept a consensus view. But Ken's parents were equally influential in this respect. Old-fashioned working-class Tories they may have been, but they didn't have the traditional prejudices of their social group.

'My father spent fifteen years in the merchant navy, travelling around the world and working with all races. He opposed racism in any form, believing that people were all basically the same and should be treated equally. And my mother grew up on the stage, surrounded by gays, and by a degree of individual sexual freedom which was not acceptable outside the theatre. So my father gave me a sound view on race, and my mother gave me a sound view on sexuality. There was a climate of tolerance in my house. The parents of my contemporaries at school were nothing like that.'

An early childhood ambition was to be a 'spaceman' (this was in the days before the word 'astronaut' was coined), largely because of the 1950s radio series *Journey Into Space*, a favourite of his. 'It was a very good series, but full of dreadful class stereotypes. And I wanted to be the main character – Jet Morgan. Now Jet, of course, was played by an actor called Andrew Faulds, who today is a *very* right wing Labour MP. We laugh about it sometimes – I mean, here we are, at opposite ends of the Labour spectrum, and he was my child-hood hero. He threatens to sue whenever I tell the story.

'As the weediest and runtiest kid in school, I was dreadful at sports. Naturally, you have no interest in something in which you always fail. As I was so small, I had to live on my wits and develop my verbal skill and sense of humour.'

His overriding passion during adolescence was for his collection of exotic reptiles and amphibians, which he bought with his pocket money and his earnings as a paper boy. His bedroom was like the reptile house at the zoo. The family's favourite was Black Joe, a South American bullfrog, which Ken took for walks on his shoulder, to shock people. He also owned a pair of three-foot long monitor lizards, some sala-manders, snakes and a baby alligator. He often crept out at night to dig in neighbours' gardens for worms to feed to his pets, having exhausted the worm population of his own garden.

Once he looked after two extremely poisonous Formosan vipers for a friend who went away on holiday. The friend had generously provided a serum which, in case someone was bitten, had to be injected within two minutes in order to prevent death.

At eighteen he briefly had a political hero: Harold Wilson, who became leader of the Labour Party in 1963. 'He was an incredibly predominant and successful figure who wowed an entire generation.' Ken assumed that Wilson would trans-form Britain, but he was to be bitterly disillusioned.

At twenty-five, intending to become a teacher, Ken got a

teacher's certificate, but not long afterwards he became active in local politics and 'fell in love with local government'. It was when he joined the old Greater London Council that his political ambitions really took off, and at the age of thirty he decided to become a full-time politician.

'Things have changed so much. I picked things up from my parents and other adults around me, now young people pick them up directly from television. The news flow from television is stunning. A ten-year-old child today gets more information about what's happening in the world than, say, the Archduke Franz Ferdinand would have done in the run-up to World War I. Kids develop the ability to filter and assemble that information in their own minds. They grow up so much more *aware*. I walk along the streets of my constituency and little kids call out, "Ooh, look, there's Red Ken – our MP!" I didn't even know what an MP *was* at that age.'

He has an unequivocal message for young rioters and anarchists: 'Go and educate yourselves. Generations of working-class kids have gone to evening classes and things like that. They've dragged themselves up. Also, get involved in the local power structures, join your local labour party, stand for your council, stand for Parliament – start running the machine. You won't get anywhere by burning it down, because you just burn down your own bits. That's not progress.

'If somebody like me can get to Parliament, anyone can.'

Penelope Lively, OBE

'Probably because it was an all-girls school, there was an absolute obsession with boys and men. Aside from the Royal family, this was the main topic of conversation.'

Born Penelope Low in Cairo, Egypt on 17 March 1933. Education: Private governess; an English boarding school; St Anne's College, Oxford. Career: Award-winning novelist and children's writer. Books for children include: *The Ghost of Thomas Kempe, A Stitch in Time, The Revenge of Samuel Stokes, The Stained Glass Window, Boy Without a Name, Uninvited Ghosts, A House Inside Out.*

I had a peculiar, solitary childhood in Egypt. I was an only child and I didn't attend school, because apparently there weren't any suitable schools for me to go to, so I was taught at home by the English governess who came out to look after me from the age of six months. Lucy was lovely, I was devoted to her, and she became my closest companion.

'She wasn't a trained governess or highly educated herself; she'd left school at fifteen. So she administered a kind of "do-it-yourself education kit" which had been sent out to us from England, together with timetables and instructions. We more or less learnt together.

'The whole emphasis of that teaching system was on narrative and language. I was constantly listening to stories and then having to put them into my own words. It was a marvellous discipline in the use of language; I couldn't imagine better training for a writer. Although it was distinctly short on science and maths.

'I didn't often play with children. We lived in a large, rather isolated house in the countryside outside Cairo. Once a week we'd go into the city and I'd see other children in an expatriates' club, but my only real chum was Ibrahim, our gardener's apprentice, a boy of about my age. He was employed to do the most menial tasks, like sweeping leaves, but actually he didn't seem to do much work at all. We'd meet secretly in remote parts of the garden, where he taught me Egyptian versions of hopscotch and other games, and we climbed trees. I learnt some Arabic from him, too.

'I remember being distressed by the terrible poverty all around us. There was a mud village down the road, inhabited by peasant farmers. The average life expectancy was forty, there were so many fatal diseases, and the native children looked like little ghosts. These early sights contributed to my later, left-of-centre political leanings.

'The bane of my life were the gamooses – water buffaloes – of which I was terrified. They looked fierce, with great sweeping horns, and were always tethered by a frayed rope that seemed ready to snap with one pull. They appeared to me as big as houses, but I now know that they're quite small, and the most placid of creatures. I was also alarmed by the semi-wild pi-dogs, which really *were* pretty fierce, and of course there was rabies, so all dogs and cats were taboo.

'I didn't have much to do with my parents; the relationship was not at all close. My mother looked after me on only one afternoon a week, when Lucy had her half-day off. My father was a banker, working for an Egyptian bank, and a somewhat distant figure to me as a child.

'Looking back, it seems to me to have been a happy time. I was an inquisitive, thoughtful child, and I had the opportunity to think and explore the natural world without too many intrusions. I had a strong awareness of living in a hugely ancient country, with the ruins, pyramids and temples. It all fed my imagination. I led a rich internal life, telling myself stories all the time, creating alternative fantasy worlds with whole pantheons of characters – but I think a lot of children do that.'

The happy years came to an end when Penelope was twelve. It was 1945, and the Second World War had just ended. Her parents divorced and she was sent to a boarding school in England. Not only had she never been to a school of any kind before, but she had never been apart from her beloved Lucy. It was traumatic. The bitter English cold (a shock to a girl who'd grown up in North Africa) was the least of her worries.

'It was a saga of discomfort. We never wore enough clothes, for a start. We wore a short tunic, together with stockings held up by a suspender belt. But the stockings didn't reach up to the tunic, so there was a yawning area of flesh which was perpetually frozen. The food was awful, too, and furthermore, we were made to do all the washing up, which was then added on to the fees as lessons in "domestic science".

'The school was all wrong for someone like me, who loved learning and books. One of the *punishments* there was to be sent to read for an hour in the library. It was a philistine place; the emphasis was completely on games – the typical "jolly hockey sticks" kind of school, except that instead of hockey we played a fiendish game called lacrosse, which I couldn't play at all and hated.

'I was bright academically and did well in exams, but the teachers seemed to penalize me for it. When I received a lot of distinctions in the school certificate, the report sent to my father would read, "What a pity Penelope cannot apply herself equally well in the games field."

'Being considered "brainy", a derogatory term, made you very unpopular amongst the girls, too. There were one or two other kindred spirits there, and we formed a little group of despised fringe people, ostracized by the school's *stars*, the dim but extrovert games-players. There was a lot of subtle psychological bullying; girls of that age can be absolutely vile.

'The other girls had a passion for collecting pictures of the Royal family, which I suppose was the equivalent of girls today collecting pin-ups of pop stars. Their favourites were Princess Margaret and Princess Elizabeth. None of this interested me (a republican even then) in the slightest.

'The headmistress was the most insensitive woman. I remember being summoned to see her when I first arrived and being told, "Your parents are divorced, Penelope, which is not a very nice thing. You're not to talk about that to the other girls." So I was made to feel that this, too, would turn me into a pariah. It was an extraordinary lack of understanding for someone in a custodial role. None of the staff were enlightened enough to realize that some of us girls were very disturbed indeed. I remember I actually enjoyed having chicken pox and measles, because when you were ill (but only then) a certain kindness "leaked out" of the Matron.

'Being brainy didn't stop me from having all the usual

131

anxieties and preoccupations of adolescent girls, wondering if I was pretty and that sort of thing. It was abnormal to be growing up without ever meeting boys of my own age. I barely spoke to a boy from the age of twelve until I went to university at eighteen, when I suddenly found myself surrounded by a sea of males.

'Probably because it was an all-girls school, there was an absolute obsession with boys and men. Aside from the Royal family, this was the main topic of conversation. As a social pariah I was never allowed into the inner circle where the most exciting conversations took place. The most popular girl in the class lived locally and was allowed to go home at weekends, so she had a boyfriend (or claimed to), and hence her status was ten miles high. We all waited with bated breath to find out what she'd done with her boyfriend on the downs over the weekend. Of course I was held in too much contempt to be given these revelations direct.

'During one term we were all confirmed, and we *all* fell in love with the local Anglican vicar responsible for our confirmation. He was young and good-looking and had a devastating effect on us thirteen-year-olds, pulsating as we were with burgeoning sexuality. The confirmed girls were allowed to attend Sunday service at his church in the village, as opposed to the uninteresting service at school. This gave us a good opportunity to get away from school and gaze at him, and at any teenaged boys who happened to be there.

'One really awful aspect of life at the school was the total lack of privacy. You could never be alone, you were forced to spend all your time with your peers. This was a real torture for me, who'd led such a solitary existence until then, and who so loved being alone with a book.'

Penelope was there until, aged sixteen, she was put into a crammer, a small and informal establishment where girls crammed for university entrance, which she liked because she was finally with other 'brainy' girls who wanted to learn. When she got to Oxford, though, she launched into a carefree social whirl. 'I was distinctly frivolous, a party girl.' Perhaps it was a reaction against the 'pariah' years.

She married soon after leaving Oxford, and began a family at twenty-four. She 'fell into' writing books when her younger child started school, never before having thought of writing as a vocation although she had written a lot of anguished poetry as an adolescent.

'Even while I was going through those miseries at boarding school I was aware that they would not last for ever. I knew I simply had to hang on, to survive, because things could only get better. My advice to anyone experiencing similar miseries is: don't feel there is anything wrong with you if you're the "odd man out". Be yourself – what and how you want to be is probably the right thing for you. If you're not the type to run with the crowd, that doesn't necessarily mean that the crowd is right. And to the children of divorced parents I would say: remember that your poor, wretched parents are having a hell of a time, too. Sometimes you can be too wrapped up in your own unhappiness to notice theirs.

'While my adolescence was quickly put behind me and overcome, my childhood in Egypt has remained with me much more vividly and powerfully. We tend to hold on to the good things and discard the bad – it's the healthy thing to do.'

Dave Prowse

'If there's one thing I've learnt from all that's happened to me, it's that nothing is impossible. You can do anything if you really put your mind to it.'

Born in Bristol on 1 July 1935. Education: Fonthill Road Secondary Modern, Infants and Juniors; Bristol Grammar School. Career: British Heavyweight Weightlifting Champion 1962–64; film and television actor 1976–1982; health and fitness expert.

s Darth Vader, the black-caped and masked villain in the *Star Wars* trilogy, and a dab hand with the 'light sabre', Dave Prowse was the very image of ruthless power and strength. Years earlier he'd been, as British Heavyweight Weightlifting Champion, effectively the strongest man in the country. But he's a kindly giant, who's never had a fight in his life: at 6 foot 7 inches tall, with biceps the size of watermelons, who'd be crazy enough to challenge him?

Yet this towering muscle-man had once been a feeble adolescent who'd spent a year lying in hospital with his leg in traction and another three years hobbling around in a calliper.

When Dave was five years old, his heavy-drinking father died of an ulcer, leaving his mother with no money, three kids to bring up and a mortgage to pay. His father had been a sheet-metal worker for the Bristol Aeroplane Company, and to make ends meet, his widow began to take in a succession of lodgers – men, young and old, who worked for the company.

Dave remembers very little of his father. His most vivid memory is of waiting by the front door for him to come cycling home from work, so that he could have a quick ride on the crossbar. Then one day his father was suddenly gone. Dave never really felt an acute sense of loss, mainly because he was still so small, but perhaps also because he's always been a 'loner'. He wasn't close either to his older sister or his younger brother, and his mother had little influence over him. Being self-contained and self-reliant was to be a big advantage to him later in life.

He didn't have close friends at Fonthill Road school (he says he's not the type to have 'mates'), but he was an extremely athletic child, very fast and good at sports, especially rugby. He first failed, then passed his eleven-plus exam, and entered Bristol Grammar School, where he struggled academically and found that his athleticism was largely undervalued.

'I remember always being ravenous, and eating huge amounts. I'd have a massive tea as soon as I got home from school – usually a whole loaf of bread sliced in half and spread thickly with butter and marmalade – then later have dinner with the lodgers, polish off any leftovers, and have some more to eat at a neighbour's house afterwards.'

At thirteen, suffering from a swollen knee, doctors diagnosed tuberculosis of the leg and he was rushed into Winford Orthopaedic Hospital, a sanatorium outside Bristol. His active days came to an abrupt end.

He spent a year in the children's tuberculosis ward, his leg permanently raised. His muscles atrophied. How does a sporty young boy cope with spending a year tied to a bed? 'I don't recall ever despairing. I read a lot, listened to the radio, and we had lessons every day from the two teachers who came to our ward. I'm a great one for making the best of things. I won't mope and think about my bad fortune. You have to weigh up the situation, study the pros and cons, and get on with it.'

He devoured the 'super' hospital food, and so he grew by leaps and bounds. He was 5 foot 9 inches when he went into hospital, and when he finally came out he was a 6 foot 3 inches fourteen-year-old, but weak and spindly. His three years afterwards wearing a calliper had its advantages: 'If you're disabled in any way, people are very sympathetic. As soon as you appear on the street, the traffic stops for you. Bus drivers see you limping along and wait patiently for you to board. It's marvellous – you get fantastic treatment.' However, as soon as the calliper came off, and he was no longer 'visibly impaired', he stopped being special and had to run for the bus just like everyone else.

He was seventeen by then, and the doctors who had originally diagnosed TB now claimed to have been mistaken all along. The year immobilized in hospital and the three years in a calliper had all been entirely in vain. Eager to put the wasted years behind him, Dave re-joined the school rugby team. At thirteen he'd been its star player. Now he became its joke.

'I was 6 foot 5 inches by now, and I could hardly bend my knee, it had been stiff for so long. Gradually I got it working and I started running again. But I was the slowest boy on the field, and everybody's target. They all wanted to jump on me and bring me down. Then, to cap it all, I was running for touch one day when I was tackled, and I crashed into the upright post, dislodging it and bringing the crossbar bang down on top of my bad knee. I lay there thinking: this is all I need.'

He turned to something completely different. Passing a newsagent's one day, he saw a magazine for body-builders, showing a musclebound blond Adonis in a skimpy bathing suit on its cover. He bought it, thus marking the first major turning point in his life. He embarked on a rigorous routine of exercises, and before long he noticed a little bump on his arm: the first muscle he'd ever had. He became obsessed with body-building, eventually spending a fortune on books and magazines and vitamin pills.

He strutted around school with his muscle-man magazines, growing broader and tougher by the day. Pity turned to respect. He'd found his metier. His 'loner' personality was a real advantage, because he never minded spending hours on his own, just training, training, training. Not for him the busy social life of most teenagers. 'To do body-building seriously, you have to be very self-centred.'

His hero was the American Steve Reeves, Mr Universe of 1950, who went on to play Hercules and other strong-man film roles. This was the figure he most wished to emulate. 'He was the great physique of the world at that time. I named my son Steve after him.'

For several years after he left school at seventeen, he would only take on jobs which afforded him enough time to train – three or four hours of weightlifting every evening. He was offered the job of chief bouncer at Bristol's Mecca dance hall, which was ideal. It was evening work only, so he could do body-building all day long. The dance hall was filled on rock 'n' roll nights with pugnacious Teddy boys, and it was Dave's job to break up fights and generally keep things under control. By this time, of course, he'd developed an awesome physique.

He sorted out hundreds of brawls, seemingly invincible himself. 'Somebody smashed a chair over my head once, during a fight, but I didn't even notice it.' He soon won a reputation for being a trouble-shooter *par excellence*, and Mecca dance halls all over the country started clamouring for his services. But he was headed for bigger things – weightlifting.

It was his success in this sport which, a few years later, gave him an entrée into film and television acting. He always played the 'heavy', the beefcake or the monster, culminating in international fame as Darth Vader.

He also became a renowned health and fitness expert, and personal trainer to the rich and famous (e.g. Edward Heath, Bianca Jagger, Gene Wilder, Albert Finney, Crown Prince Khalid of Saudi Arabia). He trained Christopher Reeve for his Superman role in 1976, putting an extra thirty pounds of solid muscle on to his chest and shoulders to create that magnificent V-shaped body.

'If there's one thing I've learnt from all that's happened to me, it's that nothing is impossible. You can do anything if you really put your mind to it. I sometimes wonder how my life would have turned out if I'd had the influence of a father. I've had to fend for myself all the way through, making every decision on my own. My father might have been stricter with my schooling, insisting that I study harder and get qualifications, or he might have wanted me to follow in his footsteps as a tinsmith. Things might have been very different if, instead of being left to my own devices, I'd had strong parental guidance.'

Then again, things might have been exactly the same. As

Dave himself admits, he's been unable to influence his own two grown-up sons. Both tall and well-built, Dave has tried to encourage them to train for athletic competition – in other words, to follow in *his* footsteps – but they're not interested. Like many young people, they've reacted against their father's values. But that doesn't seem to bother Dave. He's handled worse problems than that.

Edwina Currie, MP

'There's no point in having a probem, if you haven't got a solution.'

Born Edwina Cohen in Liverpool on 13 October 1946. Education: Moss Pits Lane County Primary, Liverpool Institute for Girls, St Anne's College Oxford, London School of Economics. Career: Teacher and lecturer until 1981; first entered local government politics in Birmingham in 1975; Conservative MP for South Derbyshire since 1983; Parliamentary Under Secretary of State for Health from 1986–88.

Edwina Currie comes from a family of Ashkenazy Jews. Her father's family emigrated from the Baltic region, and while the rest of his siblings moved on to their ultimate destination – America – her father chose to settle in Liverpool. He was trained as a tailor and worked in various factories before and during the Second World War. After the war he set up his own modest business.

Her maternal grandfather came from Poland. A veteran of the First World War (on the British side), this proud and strong-minded man was the dominant grandparent of Edwina's childhood. He insisted that his children should speak only English, no Yiddish. He and his Estonian wife were very keen on education for their children (they had ten, of whom eight grew to adulthood). The first three offspring had to go out to work (including Edwina's mother), so that the rest of them could go on to university.

Edwina had always been an intensely academic child, hard-working, disciplined, actively seeking out intellectual challenge. She won her first scholarship to the prestigious Liverpool Institute for Girls at Blackburne House, and her second to Oxford University, where she read PPE (Philosophy, Politics and Economics). Her mother was sympathetic to her higher educational aims, but her father definitely was not. 'He came from a much more *medieval* tradition, and couldn't understand why his daughter wanted to go to university, and particularly somewhere as outlandish and gentile as Oxbridge.

'Much of his approach to life was negative and fearful, wary and rather hostile. He was the only member of his whole family left behind, and he was left behind because he was too scared to go to America. He lived much of his life in a self-protective shell.' He and Edwina often argued about politics, but his refusal to vote infuriated her. How could he be interested, yet not vote? she would demand. She tried to persuade him that if he got involved and joined in, he would have some influence. But to no avail.

'Eventually I became convinced that I'd have to go into

politics myself – if people like him wouldn't, then somebody like me had to. I believe very deeply (which means that the belief must have been laid down quite young) that people have an obligation to society and to the community in which they live. That's a traditionally Jewish commitment. But growing up in Britain and being exposed to a far greater range of stimuli, and seeing what the attitude of "don't want to get involved" had done to the Jewish community, I couldn't accept this notion of standing back and just looking after our own. Now *that's* a source of conflict.'

Her father's negative influence was more than balanced out by the wholly positive influence of her headmistress at Blackburne House, the remarkable Miss Hiscock. Originally from Kent and quintessentially English, she was a learned woman who hated Liverpool, and who offered 'much bigger worlds'.

Books have always been a vital, influential part of Edwina's life. 'My favourite book as a child was Frances Hodgson Burnett's *The Secret Garden*. I was fascinated by the notion that somewhere in the wall there was a door, and you could walk through it and find a secret garden. That was immensely powerful imagery. But what began to happen as I got to secondary school, was that I was opening the door and realizing that *I* was in the secret garden, and there was a great big world out there . . . and I didn't have to *stay* in the secret garden.'

This 'secret garden' was defined by the limits of her Jewish upbringing, her working-class craftsman's background, and by Liverpool itself: a decaying city, 'letting itself die'. Miss Hiscock showed her that there were many doors, and that all one had to do was to choose one, turn the handle and walk out. Armed with a good education, you could go anywhere, you had personal strength.

'If you read good books, good novels, you've always got a private world – you've always got friends. You are never bored. If you have music, you have a universal culture. If you have an understanding of international ideas, you're an international person.'

Miss Hiscock was not a dominant character, but a quiet little woman, yet her pupils were all terrified of her. 'We didn't like her very much, because she "talked posh". She was terribly shy, and we thought she was being superior. So I don't think she had much influence on most of the girls, but she ran a good little school, and *this* person, at least, she helped to escape.' It was Miss Hiscock who directed Edwina towards Oxbridge, despite her father's disapproval.

Edwina grew up fascinated by the world of politics and public affairs. Living in Liverpool, a city long past its heyday as a thriving port and fraught with endless economic and industrial problems, made her look very hard at the structure of society. Her political hero was Harold Macmillan, the great Conservative leader of the late fifties and early sixties. His positive attitude towards Europe, in particular, inspired her. He was ahead of his time, attempting to move away from the British Empire and the Commonwealth, and look to a new European future. 'He struck me as a very forward-looking, practical, innovatory character. He was very impressive.'

She made her first speech aged fourteen in a school debate, organized by the geography teacher, on whether or not Britain should join the European community. 'All these clever, socialist, Labour sixth-form girls were saying "No, we shouldn't join *them*," and I was incensed! The teacher asked if anyone would speak in favour of Europe and I cried out, "*I'll* make a speech – *I* think we should be in there!" '

She had always been told as a child that she must not 'marry out' of the Jewish faith, that she mustn't risk leaving the community, because she would be persecuted. 'But I went out, and I wasn't. And I realized that one of the things that kept that community together was fear of the outside. Now, if you remove that fear, what happens to the community? I remember arguing with the rabbi when I was about sixteen, and saying, "I hear what you're frightened of, but what do you *believe* – how should we live together?" '

When she was twenty-five Edwina became engaged to

Ray Currie, whom she describes as 'quiet and undemonstrative, very Northern European, a Viking, a big, solid, blond chap with a moustache'. In other words, about as non-Jewish as you can get. She told Ray that her father would never accept him, and he said, 'Codswallop. I'll go and talk to him.' He came back white and shaken, and said, 'You're dead right.' Edwina asked, 'What do we do?', to which he replied, 'I think we just go ahead. We've signed the mortgage, we've bought the puppy, let's just go.'

Edwina never saw her father again. He refused to attend the wedding and wouldn't let the rest of the family attend, either. He died four years later, without ever having seen his granddaughter.

She was not distressed or embittered by this family rift, because she had known for a long time that she was bound to marry someone who didn't suit her father. 'There was no point in feeling anything about it,' she says, adding matter-of-factly, 'There's no point in having a problem, if you haven't got a solution.'

How does Edwina perceive herself today? 'I'm centre-right, and I know, contrary to the way I was brought up, that my beliefs are widely shared by people from a vast variety of cultures. People can live decent, honourable, kindly lives without having to belong to the Ashkenazy community.' She gave as an example the old mining community in her Derbyshire constituency: the strong sense of shared lives, the teamwork, the mutual commitment and trust within a terribly dangerous all-male industry, the caring attitude towards widows and pensioners, the passion for education as the only alternative to a life in the pits. These values were a great contribution to British life, and the values lived on, despite the closure of the pits and the emergence of a new post-industrial era. The Jewish community has likewise made valuable contributions to our society, and it needn't be afraid that, through greater integration these would be lost.

One lesson, learnt in childhood, has stood her in particularly good stead in adult life: 'Not to waste time, but to use it as wisely as possible – which involves the self-discipline I mentioned earlier. This also has its disadvantages, though. I'm not very good at going to the smoking room here at the House of Commons and having a drink and chatting up my colleagues. But I know I should, and I think I would have been more successful if I had. To me, having a drink and a chat is a waste of time. But in British politics, in the male-dominated Commons, it isn't – it's part of the mainstream activity.'

But the importance of the lesson remained undiminished. She had learnt it at school – from women teachers intent on getting good education into teenage girls and nagging them into using their education – and from the simple fact of being a girl herself. She knew she had to be as good as the boys, or better. 'You couldn't fail. If you failed, you'd end up married with six kids – there are thousands of women like that in Liverpool. So you get on with it, and use your time as well as possible.

'I would advise kids today to do two things: serve their community – which they can translate as broadly as they like: whether it's Europe, or the UK, or Leeds, or our street or our club or whatever. And secondly, look after themselves – preserve and maintain whatever talents they've got, and their health. Whatever they have been given they should keep in good order and not abuse, and turn it to the service of other people. And I think most of them do.'

Susan Hampshire

'When it was my turn to stand up in class and read aloud (Shakespeare was the worst), I'd take the hamster out and put her down on the table in front of me. This immediately distracted everyone.'

Born in South Kensington, London on 12 May 1942. Education: The Hampshire School, Knightsbridge, London. Career: Actress. Films include: *Living Free, David Copperfield, Night Must Fall*. Plays include: *The King and I, Blithe Spirit, A Little Night Music*. TV work includes: *The Forsyte Saga, Vanity Fair, The Pallisers, The First Churchills, The Barchester Chronicles*. Winner of three Emmy Awards for Best Actress.

Susan Hampshire owes a great deal to a wise and understanding mother. By the time Susan was of school age, it was clear to Mrs Hampshire that her third daughter had some sort of nameless disability which would make it extremely difficult for her to learn in a conventional school setting.

With remarkable shrewdness and originality, she decided to establish a school herself, purely so that she could take Susan under her wing educationally and give her the best possible chance in life. That disability has since acquired a name and a high profile: dyslexia, 'word blindness'. Her mother was so quick to spot it because she was herself dyslexic, although she never acknowledged it.

She opened the school when Susan was five, having previously run a dancing school. So their first classroom was a converted ballet studio with mirrored walls, making it seem as though there was a big crowd of children, instead of the mere handful. The school was to become a great success, and some of Susan's classmates gained eminence later in life, e.g. the ballet dancers Anthony Dowell and Maina Gielgud.

'I have two much older sisters; we've always been very close and it was almost like having three mothers. They all gave me an enormous amount of attention and love, I was nurtured along and was able to develop confidence and self-esteem, despite my terrible problem with reading and writing. God knows how I would have fared in life if I'd had to survive in the ordinary school system. I was still having trouble spelling my name at the age of nine. I had enormous difficulty reading anything aloud even at twelve.

'My mother was very encouraging; she taught me to find my strengths and learn to cope with my handicap. She instilled in me a positive attitude to life – perhaps the greatest gift one can give. From my father (who separated from my mother at about the time I was born) I inherited great determination and single-mindedness and the ability to work hard. I believe it's the combination of all these things which has enabled me to forge an acting career despite my dyslexia.'

Despite being in her mother's school, Susan had to devise her own, highly original means of survival. There was obviously no way in which she could compete academically with her schoolmates. Yet she desperately wanted to do well and win their approval, and most importantly – to be liked.

'I befriended the cleverest children in the class, was always very nice to them and their parents, and so when it came to homework, they could hardly refuse to let me copy from them, or to do it for me altogether. In return, I'd buy them either sweets or little glass animals (which were all the rage then) with money I'd pilfer from my mother's handbag.

'I suppose it was bribery, but there was nothing deliberate or planned about it, it was *instinctive*, it came from the gut, a self-protection mechanism. In the end, my mother had to sleep with her handbag under her pillow. But even that didn't stop me. I'd get up at five-thirty in the morning and carefully remove the bag, take out the equivalent of about ten pence, then put the bag back. I'd stop off in the shops on my way to school to purchase my little presents. This went on until I was about fourteen. I never really considered it *stealing*; it was just a necessary part of my survival.

'Another ruse was to make myself different and amusing at school. Sometimes, before leaving the house in the morning, I'd grab my hamster Whiskatina and put her into my cardigan pocket. When it was my turn to stand up in class and read aloud (Shakespeare was the worst), I'd take the hamster out and put her down on the table in front of me. This immediately distracted everyone. Whiskatina would be munching on the food I'd brought along for her, stuffing her cheeks, and then cleaning her whiskers with tiny pink paws. The whole class would fall about laughing, having forgotten all about my reading. The teacher, who knew how painful it was for me to read, often indulged me in this. Whiskatina's performance usually went on until the bell rang and we moved on to another class.

'Every seven weeks or so Whiskatina produced a few baby hamsters, and I'd take them into school (on the days when I had the most difficult lessons) and sell them for a shilling each. This was another effective method of distraction.

'I also made myself liked by offering to do messy and unpopular jobs – sweeping the floor after lunch, putting away chairs, stacking books, helping the smaller children. And I was always eager to set a good example in all the classes in which I was not hopeless, such as singing and games. But again, it was all done instinctively – not by design.'

One day when Susan was eight, she was travelling on the underground with her mother, when they chanced upon a friend who worked in the film business and was then searching for a young girl to play in a film called *Woman in the Hall*. Susan seemed perfect for the role, was given a screen test and offered the part.

'Making that film gave me a great sense of achievement. It also gave me a taste of another kind of life – the adult, working life, which I found exhilarating. I was dreadfully spoilt, being driven to Pinewood Studios early each morning in a luxurious car, and treated as a grown-up. I was *asked* my opinion about things, not told what to do. And the stars, Jean Simmons and Ursula Jeans, were very sweet to me.

'That film didn't lead to any other roles; it wasn't intended to. My mother didn't want me to become a "child star", to send me to stage school or acquire an agent. But that first, thrilling experience of the film world stayed with me and I longed to return to it one day.'

Mrs Hampshire, who'd been a professional dancer with the D'Oyly Carte Opera in her youth, hoped that Susan, too, would become a ballerina. But by her mid-teens she'd grown too tall for the classical ballet. Susan's other passion was for nursing, but realizing that she could never get the required O level in Latin, that idea, too, was reluctantly dismissed.

'I remember asking my father, when I was fifteen, whether

he'd lend me some money so that I could buy myself a pair of stockings. He turned to me and said, "I earn my living; you earn yours". He didn't mean it unkindly. But anyway, that's when I decided to become an actress. My parents disapproved, especially my father. He was a highly success-ful business executive living in the north of England, and wanted me to go to university and have some sort of aca-demic career. To him, acting wasn't a serious occupation, it was just a waste of time. But with the stubbornness and arrogance of youth, I disregarded his wishes.

'With the help of my brother-in-law, I wrote a hundred letters to repertory companies throughout the country. I received one reply, offering me a job as assistant stage man-ager (with small acting parts) at the Roof Garden Theatre, Bognor Regis. The pay was six pounds ten shillings per week.

'A few years later, when I became noticed and was getting good parts in films and the West End theatre, and the news-papers published stories about me (especially in the gossip columns), my father was embarrassed by all the attention. He told my mother I'd have to change my name and "get rid of that blonde hair". It's a source of sadness to me that both my parents died before I made my real breakthrough – in *The Forsyte Saga*.'

In between acting jobs Susan supported herself in any way she could. Once, she was delighted to be offered a well-paid six-week engagement as 'commentator' for a knitwear fashion show. Her job entailed sitting at a desk and reading out descriptions of the knitwear being modelled, to an audi-ence of department store buyers. On the first day she was handed twenty closely typed pages of commentary; she panicked.

Her opening line was, 'Good morning, ladies, and wel-come to Braemar's Spring Collection.' This she read out as, 'Good morning, ladies and gentlemen. I hope you enjoy the collection – it's boring . . . er, I mean Braemar.' She went on: 'This beautifully soft jumper in push cashmere has tribbed ruffs – I mean ribbed cuffs – and it's both sparky and tart . . . er, smart and sporty.'

She made one ghastly mistake after another. The models were convulsed with laughter and the buyers were astounded, especially as Susan kept reversing the digits in the reference numbers and prices. But she didn't get the sack. No fashion show had ever been so amusing and memorable. She was complimented on her humour and freshness of style, and instructed to keep the mistakes in.

Many people with severe dyslexia would have found the task of reading and memorizing lines – a major part of any actor's work – virtually insurmountable. But the problem seemed to give Susan an added incentive to get on and succeed. 'I wanted to blot out the memory schoolfriends must have had of me struggling to read Shakespeare, and put a new image in their minds, of someone they could like, perhaps even respect and admire.

'As you grow older, you cloud over those things in your life which you wish to forget, and remember only what you want to remember. I can no longer recall clearly the horrendous struggle of going for job after job after job and not being able to read the scripts I was given – the sheer humiliation of it all. I only remember that I had good luck; long before I was twenty-one I was starring in the West End with my name in lights. I'd managed, despite everything, to get the role. I have survived.'

Bruce Oldfield, OBE

'I wanted to be a *star*. I wanted to be recognized for something.'

Born in Hammersmith, London, on 14 July 1950. Education: Dean Bank Infant and Junior School, Spennymoor Grammar School (Durham), Ripon Grammar School, Sheffield Polytechnic, Ravensbourne College of Art, St Martin's College of Art. Career: Fashion designer since 1973; set up his own business in 1975; opened his London shop in 1984. Private clients include the Princess of Wales, Charlotte Rampling, Diana Rigg, Joan Collins and Jerry Hall.

Bruce Oldfield knows very little about who his parents were. 'I was illegitimate. My mother was a white, working-class woman called Betty Eileen Oldfield. Apparently she was an itinerant factory worker, and I know she was a packer in an electric light bulb factory at some point, because that's what it says on my birth certificate. She couldn't look after me, so when I was about a week old the Salvation Army took me. And from there I was handed on to Dr Barnardo's.'

According to his case file, his father was a Jamaican boxer, name unknown. But Bruce is sceptical. 'I think he must have been an Arab. Arabs are always taking me for one of them – Egyptians, Tunisians, Lebanese, etc. – and speaking to me in Arabic. And *I* think I look more like an Arab than a Jamaican. I don't know – it's a mystery to me.'

Once or twice he thought he'd like to solve this mystery, to pursue the matter and find out just who his father was. But he'd quickly lose interest in it. 'I don't have a burning desire to know.' He has no idea whether his mother is still alive, but he doubts it. For nearly two decades he has been a highly publicized personality in the fashion world, and if she were still alive she'd have come forward by now.

Aged six months he was taken north to a Dr Barnardo's nursery home in Harrogate, and shortly afterwards put into the care of a foster-mother, Violet Masters. 'Aunty Vi' was to play a vital, decisive role in his life.

She was a spinster, very poor, of indeterminate age ('She always lied about her age'), a white woman who chose to foster mainly black kids. She had a whole group of them at once – 'Besides me there was Barry, who was half-Nigerian, and Linda, who was half-Ceylonese, and her younger half-sister Janet, who was half-Jamaican . . .'

It was a happy household, but very poor. They lived in a small terraced house on the A1 in Durham – two up, two down – with a primitive loo in the back yard. Aunty Vi was a dressmaker, and even as a small child Bruce found that an

absorbing occupation. She couldn't afford to buy clothes for
her small charges, especially in those austere post-war days
when rationing was still in effect. So she made clothes for
them instead. And she taught them how to sew and weave
and knit. Bruce was, as he puts it, 'a bit of a sissy', who
liked playing with dolls and messing around with all her
dressmaking things.

He says that although she was very caring, she wasn't the
most intelligent of women. Yet when, ten years ago, he went
to the Essex headquarters of Dr Barnardo's to look up his
file, he found a report dated 1957 (when he was seven years
old) which said, 'Foster mother believes boy will be a fashion
designer'. That shows not only intelligence, but downright
clairvoyance.

He was thirteen when he left Aunty Vi's house. Why? 'I
was a bad boy. I was out of control.' It was the 'rebellious
teenager' syndrome, the oldest story in the world. He had
engaged in a little mischievous schoolboy shoplifting,
although he was never in trouble with the police: 'I was too
smart for that.

'What always used to madden us was the way we had to
live with constant threats hanging over us. When you're
fostered out they say, "Behave yourself or you'll get sent
back to the home". When you're in the home it's, "Behave
yourself or you'll be made a ward of court", or, "Behave
yourself or you'll be sent to borstal". Even then I felt that
that was very inappropriate child psychology; you can't have
children living under threat like that.

'Violet was part of that whole system, too, and so when
I grew too hot to handle, she sent me back to Barnardo's,
and they put me into one of their homes. I can't really blame
her; she was a single woman, there was no man there to
take control, and I was a big boy even at that age, at least as
big as she was. Bringing me up must have been a frustrating
job, especially as she was already about sixty years old.'

He didn't calm down at the Barnardo's home in genteel,

middle-class Ripon, a far cry from rough, depressed, working-class Durham. Bruce kicked against the regimentation of institutional life, at its many petty rules and what he saw as its injustices. However, he was always treated as a special case – in the nineteen sixties, of the many thousands of youngsters in the care of Dr Barnardo's, only a tiny handful were going to grammar school, and Bruce was one of them. He was a rebel with brains, who applied himself at school.

'The grammar school was situated directly opposite the secondary modern school, and there was great antagonism between the two. The grammar school kids were seen as snobs, and the secondary modern kids as louts. The superintendent of the home I lived in had a son going to the secondary modern school, and he was not exactly chuffed at the fact that *I* was at the grammar school. So we got on to rather a bad footing.'

Nevertheless, the move to Ripon was, he says, the best thing that could have happened to him. The attractive, historic market town was a more spiritually uplifting place in which to live. Even as a youngster he could appreciate its tree-lined streets and elegant architecture. His new home was a Georgian mansion set in its own grounds, and his new school was of a much higher academic standard, which made him set his own sights higher.

'I stuttered badly throughout my childhood and adolescence, which really complicated school life. More than anything, I always dreaded having to read aloud in class. It was totally, totally mortifying. Especially later, when it came to A level French.' In fact, stuttering was his *real* social handicap, not being parentless and illegitimate.

He had an abiding interest in clothes. In art class at school, he always drew pictures of women wearing the latest styles. It was the mid-sixties – the Beatles and other Liverpool pop groups were rocking the world with their 'Mersey beat', and London, with its bright and brassy Carnaby Street, and Mary

Quant's boutique on the King's Road, was the international centre of fashion. Twiggy, the star model, was the great cultural icon. There were two rival youth cults – the Mods and the Rockers, and amongst the hit tunes of the era was one called *Dedicated Follower of Fashion* – 'It might as well have been written about me.'

Although he no longer lived with her, the crucial bond with Aunty Vi was not broken: he was allowed to stay with her during school holidays, when she helped him make trendy clothes for himself. 'I remember returning to Ripon after one holiday wearing a flowered shirt and purple striped trousers. The superintendent was appalled. "That's fine for the beach!" he said. But we never went to the beach.'

He frequented the Underworld, a racy coffee bar in Ripon that was declared strictly off-limits by Barnardo's. He kept his stylish homemade gear stashed away there, changing into it when he arrived. At sixteen he was nipping out of his bedroom window at night and hitch-hiking into Harrogate or Leeds, going to clubs and discos, and sneaking back into the home at four in the morning. 'My A levels would have been better had I not been doing that sort of thing, but there you go.'

He had a false start after school at Sheffield Poly, where he did a three-year teacher training course. He'd never wanted to be a teacher; it was the idea of his former head-mistress at Ripon Grammar School. But while there he managed, 'miraculously', to cure himself of his stutter. He'd decided to run for the office of social secretary of the students' union, and at the hustings, had to get up and give a speech to the assembled student body. 'The shock of being thrust into the limelight forced the stutter right out of me. I was elected to the office, which greatly boosted my self-confidence. I also discovered that I had a definite liking for the limelight.

'I did a lot of art and design at the Poly, which made me realize once and for all that my true vocation was a creative one and that, come what may, I simply had to get into art school. I wanted to be a *star*. I wanted to be recognized for something.' Dr Barnardo's was predictably dismissive of this errant ambition, but Bruce was 'arrogant and pushy' enough to persist.

At the home they had always tried to stamp out individualism and daring. 'I remember they were always saying to me, "Who do you think you *are*?" (I had a great facial vocabulary of sneers, for which I was always getting into trouble.) The problem was, they never expected you to make much of your life, and they tried to drill those low expectations into you.' With Bruce, they didn't succeed. 'Throughout my life whenever I've been told, "You can't do it", I'd say "Tut-tut – of course, I can!" '

Barnardo's agreed, in the end, to give him the necessary grant for art school. And when, at the age of twenty-five, he set up his own business, they gave him the £500 loan he required. He acknowledges the debt he owes, and today supports the organization by raising funds for it through his special gala evenings, attended by his most prestigious client, HRH The Princess of Wales. 'Barnardo's have a much more enlightened attitude towards youngsters now than they did in the fifties and sixties, when I was growing up.'

He kept in touch with his far-sighted foster-mother, Violet Masters, until her death in 1974, when he was on the brink of real success. He owes to her not only his original inspiration as a dress designer, and his early knowledge of the craft, but also the fact that he does have a 'family' today: he has remained close to the assorted 'foster-siblings' with whom he grew up in her care. As he is unmarried and childless, they are the only family he has.

Institutional life does not encourage individuals to make stars of themselves. It is designed to make the individual conform to a system, to blend unobtrusively into a given order. In his determination to be different and make a name for himself, he was following his instincts. That yearning to succeed, to 'make it big', came not from any outside influence, but from within himself – it was, as they say, 'in the genes'. In other words, he owes a considerable debt, also, to Betty Eileen Oldfield and to his father – whoever he was, and wherever he came from.

Monica Porter

'A person can be many things, and belong to many places.'

**Born Mónika Halász in Budapest, Hungary on 25 July 1952.
Education: Public school 122, Bronx, New York City; Woodlands
High School, Hartsdale, New York; Webber-Douglas Academy
of Dramatic Art, London. Career: Journalist, author and
broadcaster.**

I come from an immigrant family. I was four when we left Hungary, just after the Uprising was crushed, and started a new life in America. My mother was a singer and actress, and my father was a writer. It's not very imaginative of me, but my own two ambitions have been, first of all, to act, and secondly, to write. I suppose you could say my parents have influenced me.

But that came later. To begin with, growing up in America, I just wanted to be like all the other kids around me. It wasn't easy. People mispronounced my surname. We ate *paprikás krumpli* instead of hamburgers. At Christmas we were told about angels bringing us presents; that fat guy called Santa Claus who flies around with reindeer was a big nobody in our home.

I desperately wanted to be a real product of Yankee culture. In the playground I'd invent all-American names for myself, like 'Gail Brown'. Once I said my father was a sergeant in the US Army; it sounded good until he turned up in a tweed jacket, smoking a pipe . . . some sergeant.

After a while I became that dreaded creature: the rebellious teenager. All my girlfriends were doing the liberal American sixties thing – going steady, throwing pyjama parties, talking on the phone for hours – but I couldn't do any of that. My parents were strict and intent on protecting me from these 'undesirable' influences. So I fought back. Once I even ran away. But the next day, with no money left, I went home. It was cold and rainy and I felt forlorn.

I changed after that. It was a real turning point for me. Humiliated by my defeat, I gave up such futile acts of defiance. Instead, I channelled my energies into planning for the future, and a career on the stage.

During my last year at high school I performed in several plays and won the drama award. By then I knew I was going to study acting in London and I couldn't wait to get to the great metropolis. I was sick of suburban New York.

I flew to London on my eighteenth birthday. Being in Europe once more made me feel closer to my cultural background, which was becoming increasingly interesting to me. As a kid I'd wanted only to conform, but now I began to revel in everything which set me apart – like being an ex-refugee who'd survived Russian tanks and Molotov cocktails and minefields.

After drama college I joined a touring company and played the title role in a pantomime called *The Princess Who Couldn't Laugh*. And I really didn't laugh much that winter: we travelled in the back of a freezing van, the scenery and costumes falling on top of us at every sharp turn. I wrote an article about it for *The Stage*. I'll never forget my wild dash to the newsagents to buy a copy and seeing, for the first time, my work in print. Every writer will tell you – it's a thrill never to be matched again.

From acting I turned to full-time writing. I'd written reams of stuff as a youngster, poems, stories, plays and even an 'autobiography' which I began when I was about six and added a little to each year: an original method, I thought. My father gave me my first little portable typewriter when I was ten. I still have this treasured memento of childhood, my equivalent of the bedraggled teddy bear or one-eyed doll.

I planned to get a writing job on a magazine. People warned me about the obstacles: I wasn't English, I hadn't been to university, I had no useful connections. Fortunately, hard-nosed editors know that, in the writing business, one really good story is worth more than an Oxbridge degree, and I'd had a few published by then. My three-year stint as staff writer on the venerable *Local Government Chronicle* was my 'university course'. I learnt the basics there from a traditional, cigar-chomping boss.

My first book, published a few years later, was about a visit to Hungary to seek out my roots and to answer finally the question: am I still, after all these years in the West, attached to my birthplace? The answer was yes. But by then I had a son who was undeniably English, and London was my home. Although a part of me will be a Yankee to the bitter end, I know now that a person can be many things, and belong to many places.

Jim Naughton
My Brother Stealing Second £3.50

Stealing second is baseball talk, and Bobby loved baseball and his brother Billy more than anything. But Billy is dead, killed in a car crash, and everything in Bobby's life has changed. He knows he's in a mess, but does it really matter any more?

Two things show him it does: the beautiful Annie Dunham, whose parents died in the same crash, and the incredible truth about what really happened that night. At last, he knows exactly what he's got to do . . .

'Naughton hits a home run on every page . . . *My Brother Stealing Second* is a grand-slam book' THE WASHINGTON POST

Will Gatti
Absolute Trust £3.50

The Bureau of Internal Affairs August 6, 1999

To: All Agents Confidential

Suspect arrives Heathrow, 1200 GMT. Full surveillance authorised.

Britain was no longer the place for an easy holiday. These days people disappeared there. And elections and free speech were a thing of the past.

Not that Jeremiah Talent was worried. He was smart. People liked him. And besides, didn't everyone know that his father was the US Ambassador?

But the wrong people had heard about Jeremiah Talent.

And now they were going to teach him a thing or two about fear . . .

Robert Westall
The Promise £3.50

Valerie was beautiful, with her long red hair and pale, pale face. Bob found it easy to promise – that he'd come and find her if she ever got lost. A boy in love will do anything he's asked. It seemed such a little thing at the time.

But he'd underestimated Valerie. Used to having her own way in life, she was no different in death. She still wanted Bob, pulled him ever closer to the brink. While the bombs of World War II rained down, Bob faced Valerie in a final test of will – with his own life at stake.

Mary Wesley
The Sixth Seal £3.50

Pink and green snowfalls in July are just the first in a series of disturbing incidents worldwide – until a deadly storm blasts the life out of everything it touches.

Only a few people remain, like Muriel, her son Paul and his friend Henry, who are below ground when the storm strikes. Stranded in the Devon countryside, they band together with other survivors to make the most of their strange new world.

Inevitably, tensions rise and Henry leaves for London – and a bizarre confrontation in the Cabinet room of 10 Downing Street. Muriel and Paul set off in pursuit – and find themselves at the mercy of a nightmare city . . .

All Pan books are available at your local bookshop or newsagent, or can be ordered direct from the publisher. Indicate the number of copies required and fill in the form below.

Send to: Pan C. S. Dept
            Macmillan Distribution Ltd
            Houndmills Basingstoke RG21 2XS
or phone: 0256 29242, quoting title, author and Credit Card number.

Please enclose a remittance* to the value of the cover price plus: £1.00 for the first book plus 50p per copy for each additional book ordered.

*Payment may be made in sterling by UK personal cheque, postal order, sterling draft or international money order, made payable to Pan Books Ltd.

Alternatively by Barclaycard/Access/Amex/Diners

Card No.

Expiry Date

Signature:

Applicable only in the UK and BFPO addresses

While every effort is made to keep prices low, it is sometimes necessary to increase prices at short notice. Pan Books reserve the right to show on covers and charge new retail prices which may differ from those advertised in the text or elsewhere.

NAME AND ADDRESS IN BLOCK LETTERS PLEASE:

....

Name_____

Address_____

_____

_____

_____

6/92